I0169946

Born Again?

What's Next?

Born Again? What's Next?

Vinu V Das

TP
Tabor Press

© 2025 Tabor Press. All rights reserved. No part of this publication may be reproduced, distributed, or transmitted in any form or by any means without the prior written permission of the publisher, except in the case of brief quotations embodied in critical reviews and certain other noncommercial uses permitted by copyright law.

978-0-9940194-5-5

Table of Contents

Introduction

The journey of faith does not end at salvation; in many ways, it has only just begun. The moment a person is born again, a radical transformation takes place—a new identity is formed, a new path is set, and a new purpose unfolds. However, many believers find themselves asking, *What happens next? How do I grow in my faith? What does it truly mean to live as a follower of Christ?*

This book is written for those who desire more than just the title of "Christian"—for those who long to walk in the fullness of what it means to be born again. It is an invitation to move beyond passive belief into active discipleship, beyond spiritual infancy into maturity, and beyond a self-focused faith into a Christ-centered mission.

In many ways, the Christian life is like stepping into a vast, uncharted territory. While the joy of salvation is real and transformative, the road ahead presents challenges, decisions, and responsibilities. How do we align our lives with the will of God? How do we navigate trials, temptations, and spiritual battles? How do we live in a world that often opposes the very truth we now embrace?

This book does not merely provide theological insights but also practical wisdom for walking this path with conviction and purpose. It explores the nature of true faith, the power of transformation, and the daily battles that every believer must confront. Through scriptural foundations, biblical examples, and real-life applications, this book equips you to grow in your relationship with Christ, live out your faith boldly, and embrace your God-given calling.

You will be challenged to examine your faith, refine your priorities, and deepen your commitment to Christ. You will discover the difference between passive Christianity and active discipleship, between mere survival and radical surrender, between following from a distance and walking in intimate fellowship with God. The choice before you is not simply whether to be a believer, but whether to be fully *alive* in Christ—whether to settle for mediocrity or pursue the abundant life He has promised.

No matter where you are in your journey, whether a new believer seeking direction or a seasoned Christian longing for renewed passion, this book serves as a guidepost for the next steps. The Holy Spirit is calling you into deeper waters, into greater faith, and into a life that bears lasting fruit for the kingdom of God.

Are you ready to go beyond salvation and into the life God has prepared for you? If so, let this book be a roadmap for the incredible journey ahead.

Chapter 1: Are You Truly Born Again? A Call to Examine Your Faith

Being "born again" is one of the most foundational concepts in Christianity, yet it is also one of the most misunderstood. The Bible conveys the idea that those who believe in Christ are not merely influenced by spiritual teachings but are profoundly changed at the core of their being, much like a new birth. Because of the importance of this transformation, it is crucial that every believer ask: *Am I truly born again?* This chapter aims to guide you through an honest self-examination of your faith, helping you distinguish genuine spiritual birth from mere religious participation or emotional excitement. In doing so, you will be encouraged to explore the foundational truths of salvation, recognize the signs of genuine conversion, identify potential misunderstandings, and begin a process of ongoing reflection.

This is not a call to doubt the grace of God but rather an invitation to lay hold of it more confidently by "examining yourselves, to see whether you are in the faith" (2 Corinthians 13:5).

1.1. Foundations of Saving Faith

1.1.1 The Nature of Spiritual Birth

Understanding the concept of spiritual birth

In Scripture, Jesus introduces the language of being "born again" in His conversation with Nicodemus: "Unless one is born again he cannot see the kingdom of God" (John 3:3). Nicodemus, a learned Pharisee, struggles to understand how an adult could re-enter his mother's womb. Jesus clarifies that this new birth is not a physical event but a spiritual one—being "born of water and the Spirit" (John 3:5). This spiritual birth underscores the complete renovation of a person's life, brought about by God Himself.

To say you are *born again* implies that there was a definitive change in your life's orientation—away from sin and toward God. Natural birth marks our entry into the physical world. In parallel, the spiritual birth marks our entry into God's kingdom, giving us new spiritual eyes, new desires, and a new identity as children of God. This transformation is not the end of a journey; rather, it is the beginning of life led by the Holy Spirit.

Grace as the starting point

When we talk about saving faith, we must remember that it begins with *grace*, the unmerited favor of God (Ephesians 2:8–9). We do not earn our status as born-again believers through good works or moral excellence. Rather, God initiates this new birth out of love, granting believers a fresh start and the capacity to live in fellowship with Him. Recognizing the role of grace keeps us humble; it reminds

11

us that our identity as born-again Christians stems from God's action, not ours.

Spiritual identity and belonging

Being born again also introduces believers into a new family—the family of God. This new sense of belonging runs deeper than any earthly social group or community. In John 1:12–13, we read: "But to all who did receive Him...He gave the right to become children of God, who were born, not of blood nor of the will of the flesh... but of God." This spiritual identity has profound implications: it reshapes our values, relationships, and ultimate purpose. A genuine believer does not see himself or herself as an isolated individual but as part of a larger spiritual tapestry woven together by God's design.

A decisive break with the old

The nature of spiritual birth also involves a break with our old life dominated by sin. While we continue to wrestle with sinful impulses, the power and penalty of sin have been fundamentally challenged by the new birth. Paul expresses this idea in Romans 6:4, urging believers to "walk in newness of life" because they have been united with Christ in His death and resurrection. This decisive break from the past does not immediately eradicate all flaws, but it does set the foundation for a progressive spiritual journey, fueled by the Holy Spirit, in which the believer actively seeks holiness.

Transformation in worldview

A key indicator of the new birth is a shift in how we see reality. Where once we might have dismissed spiritual truths as insignificant, the newly born-again believer recognizes the central importance of God, Scripture, and eternity. This transformation is often accompanied by a thirst for God's Word, renewed sensitivity to sin, and an earnest desire to do God's will. This shift in worldview is integral to being born again because it signifies an internal reorientation toward the things of God and away from the self-focused lens we naturally inherit from the world.

1.1.2 Distinguishing Genuine Conviction from Mere Emotion

Emotional experiences vs. authentic conviction

It is possible to attend a moving worship service or hear a stirring sermon and feel an emotional high—perhaps even shed tears—yet not be truly born again. Emotions can be a valuable part of our relationship with God, often providing the initial wake-up call to our spiritual condition. However, genuine conviction runs deeper than a fleeting emotional response. True conviction prompts ongoing change and a realignment of priorities, resulting in lasting transformation.

Consider the parable of the sower in Matthew 13:20–21: Jesus depicts a scenario in which seeds fall on rocky soil and quickly sprout with joy, only to wither under persecution or hardship. These individuals experience a positive emotional response to God's Word, but it never takes deep root. When challenges arise, they abandon their newfound faith. This sobering illustration highlights the difference between a surface-level, emotional reaction and a deep-seated, Holy Spirit-driven conviction.

The role of the Holy Spirit in conviction

Scripture teaches that the Holy Spirit convicts us of sin, righteousness, and judgment (John 16:8). This conviction is not a vague sense of guilt; it is a divine work that leads the believer to real repentance and transformation. When a person experiences true conviction, they recognize their personal need for forgiveness and the impossibility of achieving righteousness apart from Christ. This recognition, spurred by the Holy Spirit, drives a person to the foot of the cross in humility.

Signs of lasting change

How do we differentiate true conviction from passing emotion? One key indicator is *endurance in repentance*. Genuine conviction leads to real change over time, not just a burst of fervor that fades within days or weeks. Another sign is the development of *Christlike character*. While perfection is impossible in this life, a truly born-again believer sees incremental growth in love, patience, humility, and other virtues that reflect the heart of God. These changes might be subtle but become evident as we consistently surrender to God's shaping hand.

Heart-level transformation over outward expressions

Emotional experiences are not inherently wrong; God can use them mightily in our lives. However, a person who is truly convicted by the Holy Spirit will demonstrate repentance, humility, and dedication long after the emotional moment passes. This is why Scripture often calls for *fruit* that demonstrates genuine faith. Words of remorse or bursts of passion may carry little weight if they do not lead to a deep-rooted heart transformation. Consequently, believers must continually test the authenticity of their faith, ensuring it is rooted in divine conviction rather than transient emotions.

Seeking substance over spectacle

Modern Christian culture sometimes places a heavy emphasis on dramatic worship moments, conferences, or revival meetings. While these can be catalysts for spiritual renewal, they can also create a dependency on external stimuli rather than the consistent work of the Spirit. True spiritual birth is not about chasing sensational experiences; it is about being anchored in Christ. Indeed, the emotional surge of a conference may fade, but genuine faith clings to the truth of Scripture, seeking God diligently in the quiet routines of daily life.

1.2. Evidence of New Life

1.2.1 Internal Transformation

A renewed heart

One of the key signs of being born again is an internal transformation that redefines how we think, feel, and behave. Though this chapter will not delve fully into the specifics of mind renewal (covered in later discussions), it is helpful to note that the new birth initiates a radical shift in our innermost being. We begin to view our sin with greater seriousness, desiring to root it out rather than conceal or justify it. Our affections begin to align with God's desires, and our hearts gradually shift from self-centered pursuits to God-centered motivations.

A reoriented conscience

The born-again believer experiences a newly sharpened conscience, guided by the Holy Spirit. What once felt permissible or harmless may now bring conviction. Behaviors and attitudes that were previously overlooked or rationalized are no longer tolerable in the light of the new life we have in Christ. This is not merely an inherited moral code but an internal witness that aligns us with

God's holiness (Romans 8:14–16). When a believer sins, the Holy Spirit nudges them toward confession and repentance, leading to moral and spiritual growth.

A hunger for spiritual truth

Another evidence of internal transformation is a deepened appetite for God's Word and spiritual wisdom. Before being born again, the Bible may have seemed archaic or irrelevant. After new birth, however, believers often find themselves drawn to Scripture, discovering its beauty and power. Passages that once felt confusing begin to resonate with clarity, as the Holy Spirit illuminates God's truth (1 Corinthians 2:14). This newfound hunger can manifest in a desire to study the Bible regularly, seek out biblical teaching, and engage in meaningful fellowship with other believers who share a passion for Christ.

Increased awareness of God's presence

A further indication of internal change is a growing awareness of God's presence and activity in daily life. Rather than confining "spiritual matters" to church services, the born-again believer senses God's involvement in everyday decisions, interactions, and experiences. Prayer becomes less a rigid duty and more a dynamic conversation with a loving Father. Over time, this awareness cultivates a life that is lived in continual communion with God, embracing His guidance and cherishing His fellowship in all circumstances.

A shift in personal priorities

When the Holy Spirit takes up residence in our hearts, our priorities begin to shift. We no longer measure success purely by worldly standards such as wealth, status, or comfort. Instead, we start to value the things that matter to God—compassion, justice, righteousness, service, and evangelism. Though we may still enjoy certain hobbies and interests, there is a notable movement toward investing our time and resources in activities that reflect God's character and His heart for the world. This transformation may happen gradually, but it clearly signifies that something fundamental has changed in us.

1.2.2 Observable Spiritual Fruit

The role of fruit in identifying true believers

Jesus taught that we can recognize a tree by its fruit (Matthew 7:16–20). In a similar way, a person who is truly born again will exhibit spiritual fruit that testifies to the work of the Holy Spirit in their life. While no believer can claim sinless perfection, the consistent growth of virtues such as love, joy, peace, patience, kindness, goodness, faithfulness, gentleness, and self-control (Galatians 5:22–23) is evidence that the Spirit of God is active.

Progress over perfection

It is important to clarify that spiritual fruit does not appear instantaneously or in flawless form. Instead, a born-again believer experiences progressive growth. You may see greater compassion toward others, a softening of harsh attitudes, or a deeper patience under stress than you once had. As you continue to yield to the Holy Spirit, these virtues will mature. A healthy self-examination should note this progress over time, rather than expecting instantaneous mastery of all spiritual attributes.

Influence on relationships

Another way spiritual fruit becomes evident is through a

transformed approach to relationships. Being born again reshapes the way we treat family, friends, neighbors, and even strangers. A critical or unforgiving heart is gradually replaced by patience, empathy, and a willingness to extend grace (Ephesians 4:32). In conflict situations, believers who are growing in the Spirit seek reconciliation and unity, modeling Christ's sacrificial love. This relational transformation is particularly meaningful in families, as they often witness firsthand whether the change in behavior is superficial or truly Spirit-led.

Impact on service and generosity

A person who is truly born again will often feel compelled to serve in ways that advance the kingdom of God. This service can manifest in local church ministry, missions, community outreach, or simply acts of kindness in everyday life. Generosity also flourishes in a heart that has been regenerated by Christ. The believer may sense a deep desire to support charitable causes, share resources with those in need, and contribute to the spread of the gospel. Such acts of service and generosity are tangible outworkings of a faith that is alive and guided by the Holy Spirit (James 2:17).

Consistency and authenticity

Finally, observable spiritual fruit is marked by consistency and authenticity. The born-again believer does not simply put on a show of piety for public approval, only to revert to destructive or callous behavior in private. While everyone struggles with sin, there should be a recognizable pattern of growth, guided by the Spirit. This consistency builds a credible testimony to those around us, affirming that our profession of faith is supported by a life increasingly shaped by the character of Christ.

1.3. Common Misunderstandings

1.3.1 Relying on Religious Rituals

Tradition and its limitations

Some individuals assume that participating in certain religious rituals—be they baptisms, communion, confirmations, or other sacraments—automatically confers the status of being "born again." While these practices can hold significant spiritual meaning, they are not guarantees of regeneration. For instance, baptism is an outward sign of an inward change, but if the heart has not truly turned to God in repentance and faith, the water itself does not magically save (1 Peter 3:21 clarifies that it is not merely the removal of dirt, but an appeal to God for a good conscience).

Historical or cultural Christianity

In regions with a strong Christian heritage, many people identify as believers simply because they were raised in a Christian family or culture. They may attend church out of habit, celebrate Christian holidays, and respect the Bible as a moral guide. Yet cultural Christianity alone does not equate to genuine new birth. A personal faith that humbly responds to the gospel message is necessary for regeneration. Ritual and tradition, without heart transformation, cannot bring about salvation.

Danger of external confidence

One danger in relying on religious rituals is the false sense of security they can create. A person might believe that because they have checked all the boxes—infant baptism, confirmation classes, regular church attendance—they must be in the right standing with God. But Jesus' teaching consistently emphasizes the importance of the heart's condition (Matthew 15:8–9). He calls out the Pharisees for their outward displays of religiosity while harboring hearts far from Him. Thus, religious rituals are beneficial when rooted in genuine faith, but they can be spiritually deceptive if used as a superficial veneer.

Balancing respect for tradition with personal faith

This misunderstanding should not lead believers to dismiss all forms of tradition or ritual. Many such practices can be beautiful ways of drawing nearer to God when approached with sincerity and reverence. The key is ensuring that our hope is placed not in the ritual itself but in Jesus Christ, who alone offers salvation. Observing communion, for instance, is a scriptural command to remember Christ's sacrifice (1 Corinthians 11:24–25), yet the act is meant to stir heartfelt worship, not a mechanical repetition that we think earns divine favor.

1.3.2 Confusing Church Involvement with True Conversion

Activity vs. relationship

Church involvement—serving in various ministries, attending events, volunteering for community projects—can sometimes be mistaken for authentic discipleship. While God often uses such involvement to grow and bless believers, busyness in church activities does not necessarily indicate a regenerated heart. A person could be heavily active in church life yet lack a true relationship with Christ, never experiencing the inward renewal that defines the born-again experience.

Motivations behind service

It is wise to ask ourselves: *Why am I serving or attending church events?* Is it because I desire to bring glory to God and serve His people, or do I find satisfaction in the recognition and praise of others? Is my heart genuinely aligned with the gospel, or am I merely fulfilling social expectations? While outward service can reflect a genuine love for God, it can also function as a smokescreen, concealing a lack of genuine faith behind a flurry of religious activity.

Substituting social connections for spiritual intimacy

Many churches provide a sense of community, emotional support, and social opportunities that are appealing even apart from faith commitments. People may enjoy fellowship, potlucks, music programs, and a sense of belonging, yet never truly surrender to Christ. This scenario underscores the importance of discipleship—teaching and modeling what it means to be in the right relationship with God. The born-again experience calls us into deep union with Christ, transforming us from the inside out, not merely into membership rosters or committees.

Evaluating personal fruitfulness

One practical way to avoid confusing church involvement with true conversion is to evaluate whether you are growing in spiritual fruit. Ask yourself if your love, patience, kindness, and faithfulness are increasing as you serve. Is your involvement drawing you closer to God and shaping your character, or is it perpetuating a cycle of activity without genuine devotion? By examining personal growth alongside church activity, you can better discern whether your heart is truly anchored in Christ.

1.4. Self-Examination and Reflection

1.4.1 Personal Reflection Questions

A biblical call to test oneself

Scripture exhorts believers to "examine yourselves, to see whether you are in the faith" (2 Corinthians 13:5). Far from promoting self-doubt, this command encourages us to pursue spiritual clarity and honesty. Regular self-examination can help us identify areas of growth, patterns of sin, or even the possibility that our faith is more cultural or ritualistic than transformational.

Below are some reflective questions you might prayerfully consider:

1. **Have I recognized my need for a Savior?**

2. Do I truly see myself as a sinner in need of God's mercy, or do I assume I'm "good enough" without full reliance on Christ?

3. **Is my faith primarily emotional or intellectual, or has it permeated my daily life?**

4. Does my conviction lead to real changes in behavior, priorities, and relationships, or is it something I engage only when it's convenient?

5. **Am I experiencing a progressive transformation in my character?**

6. Do I see tangible growth in patience, love, humility, and holiness over time, even if it is gradual?

7. **What role does Scripture play in my life?**

8. Is the Bible a living source of truth that shapes my decisions, or is it more of a reference book I turn to sporadically?

9. **Do I rely on religious rituals or church involvement for assurance of salvation?**

10. Am I placing my trust in external practices instead of a genuine relationship with Christ?

These questions are not meant to condemn but to guide you into deeper spiritual insight. Through prayerful and humble introspection, the Holy Spirit can illuminate areas of your heart that need realignment or perhaps confirm that you are, indeed, walking in genuine faith.

1.4.2 Accountability and Spiritual Growth

The importance of community

Self-examination is a deeply personal process, but it should not be conducted in isolation. The Christian life is designed to be lived in a community, where fellow believers can offer encouragement, guidance, and correction. James 5:16 encourages us to "confess our sins to one another and pray for one another" as part of a healthy and transformative Christian walk. By engaging in open and honest relationships with trusted Christian friends or mentors, you create an environment in which spiritual growth can flourish.

Receiving counsel and correction

Accountability involves more than merely spending time with other believers. It requires intentional openness to counsel and, at times, loving correction. This can be challenging in a culture that often promotes self-reliance and independence. However, the Proverbs frequently highlight the value of wise counsel (Proverbs 15:22). When a fellow believer, pastor, or mentor points out a sinful pattern or an area of spiritual stagnation, viewing this input through the lens of humility and gratitude is key. Their concern for your spiritual well-being can be a gift from God.

Cultivating disciplines that reinforce new life

Alongside accountability, spiritual disciplines such as prayer, fasting, meditation on Scripture, and regular worship are critical in reinforcing the changes initiated by your new birth. While the practice of disciplines does not earn salvation, it can greatly enhance our awareness of God's presence and sharpen our ability to hear the Holy Spirit. Moreover, these disciplines often work synergistically with accountability. For instance, studying Scripture in a small group or praying regularly with a friend not only fosters communal bonds but also solidifies individual spiritual growth.

Avoiding complacency

The call to self-examination remains relevant throughout a believer's life. It is easy, after a surge of early spiritual zeal, to settle into complacency. You might assume that since you once felt strong conviction or participated in meaningful ministry, you are automatically on safe ground. Yet the Bible calls for vigilance. First Peter 5:8 describes the devil as a prowling lion seeking someone to devour, suggesting that believers must remain spiritually alert. Regular accountability, coupled with honest reflection, helps keep our faith dynamic and growing.

Embracing the journey

Finally, remember that the goal of spiritual self-examination is not perfection but faithful progress. God does not ask us to measure up to an unattainable standard; He calls us to abide in Christ, where true transformation happens. By staying connected to the Vine (John 15:4–5), maintaining accountability, and practicing spiritual disciplines, we give room for the Holy Spirit to mold us. The assurance of being truly born again is not found in human effort or church tradition alone, but in a living relationship with the Savior who promised eternal life to those who believe in Him (John 3:16).

Conclusion

The question "Are you truly born again?" is not meant to unsettle your faith or fill you with fear. Rather, it is an invitation to explore the depth and authenticity of your walk with Christ. As you have seen, true spiritual birth goes beyond outward rituals, occasional emotional experiences, or church activities. It involves a transformation at the heart level—an internal renewal that manifests in ever-increasing spiritual fruit.

If you find yourself uncertain of where you stand, take time now to prayerfully reflect. Ask God to reveal any areas of confusion, complacency, or mere formality in your faith. Invite Him to affirm where genuine transformation has already taken root. Allow the Holy Spirit to guide you toward greater assurance, knowing that the goal of self-examination is not condemnation but the joyful discovery of *life in its fullness* through Jesus Christ (John 10:10).

Scripture reminds us that God is "merciful and gracious, slow to anger and abounding in steadfast love" (Psalm 103:8). He welcomes honest seekers and those who humbly acknowledge their need for His saving grace. In the chapters to come, you will gain deeper insights into repentance, regeneration, the role of the Holy Spirit, and the ongoing journey of the believer. May this initial call to examine your faith serve as a firm foundation as you embark on the next stages of your spiritual life.

Chapter 2: Repentance and Regeneration: The Heart of a New Life

Coming to faith in Christ is not merely a one-time emotional response or a decision made under social pressure. The true essence of Christian conversion is rooted in two pivotal realities: repentance and regeneration. Together, these concepts form the bedrock of our new life in Christ, highlighting both our responsibility to turn from sin and God's power to bring about an inward transformation. Whereas repentance calls us to acknowledge our wrongdoing and change our direction, regeneration refers to the divine work that gives us a new spiritual nature. These twin themes remind us that the Christian life cannot be reduced to external conformity or intellectual assent alone; it is a heart-deep experience that reorients our entire being toward God.

In this chapter, we will dive deeply into four sections: (1) Clarifying Repentance, (2) What is Regeneration?, (3) Grace and the New Birth, and (4) Living Out a Transformed Heart. By the end of this chapter, you will have a clearer understanding of why repentance is indispensable, how regeneration operates in the believer's life, how grace underpins the entire process, and what it truly means to live from a transformed heart.

2.1. Clarifying Repentance

Repentance is one of the most frequently mentioned themes in the Bible, and yet it is often misunderstood. The English word "repentance" can evoke notions of self-loathing or merely feeling sorry for one's errors. However, biblical repentance is far richer. At its core, it involves a decisive turning away from sin and a conscious turning toward God's righteousness. Far from being a punishment, repentance is an invitation to realignment with the Creator's design. Jesus began His public ministry with a call to repentance (Mark 1:15), underscoring its importance in the life of anyone who seeks genuine fellowship with God.

2.1.1 Contrition Versus Remorse

Defining contrition and remorse

At first glance, contrition and remorse might appear synonymous, as both involve sorrow for wrongdoing. Yet these two concepts differ significantly in their focus and outcome. Remorse often centers on how sin has negatively impacted oneself—an inward pity that can be laced with shame, regret, or fear of consequences. A person plagued by remorse may worry primarily about punishment or damaged reputation rather than a heartfelt concern for having dishonored God or hurt others.

Contrition, by contrast, emerges from recognizing that sin is ultimately an offense against the holiness and love of God (Psalm 51:3–4). A contrite heart does not simply regret getting caught or having to face consequences; it is genuinely grieved over having rebelled against God's will. True contrition acknowledges the deep rift that sin creates between the human heart and God's purity. King David exemplifies this in Psalm 51, where he pleads for mercy and cleansing, recognizing that his sin is first and foremost against God Himself.

Outcomes of contrition

The outcome of true contrition differs markedly from that of mere remorse. The apostle Paul explains, "Godly sorrow brings repentance that leads to salvation and leaves no regret, but worldly sorrow brings death" (2 Corinthians 7:10). Godly sorrow (contrition) produces a genuine repentance that fosters spiritual growth, healing, and restoration. Worldly sorrow (remorse) may lead to despair and self-condemnation, keeping the individual stuck in guilt without ushering them into grace and transformation.

Practical indicators

A useful self-check involves examining our motivations when we feel remorseful about sin. Ask yourself questions such as: *Am I upset because I harmed my relationship with God and others, or am I upset because of embarrassment or negative consequences?* Reflecting on these questions can help you identify whether your sorrow is God-centered (contrition) or self-centered (remorse). If contrition is present, you will sense a movement toward humility, confession, and a renewed desire to walk in obedience. If it is merely remorse, you may find yourself trapped in self-pity or bitterness, lacking the resolve to change.

2.1.2 Turning from Past Habits

A change of mind and direction

In the New Testament, the Greek word for repentance is *metanoia*, which literally means a change of mind. It suggests that genuine repentance involves a fundamental shift in how we perceive sin, holiness, and our relationship with God. This change of mind naturally leads to a change of direction—like a traveler who recognizes they are on the wrong road and makes a U-turn to head toward the correct destination. Without this pivot in direction, repentance remains little more than lip service.

Sin as a pattern, not just an event

Many people think of sin in terms of discrete actions or individual transgressions. While certain deeds are undoubtedly sinful, the biblical view of sin also encompasses entrenched patterns and dispositions in our hearts. Thus, repentance often requires renouncing habitual behaviors—gossip, lust, greed, pride, or any practice that contradicts God's truth. In Luke 3:8, John the Baptist admonishes listeners to "Bear fruits in keeping with repentance," suggesting that turning from sinful patterns should manifest in observable changes in one's lifestyle.

Practical strategies for turning away

Breaking free from past habits often requires deliberate strategy and accountability. Consider these practical steps:

1. **Identify triggers**: Reflect on the situations, relationships, or emotional states that typically lead you into sin. Awareness of these triggers helps you preemptively avoid or better

navigate tempting circumstances (1 Peter 5:8 warns believers to be sober and vigilant).

2. **Seek community support**: Confessing your struggles to mature believers or mentors can provide support, prayer, and encouragement (James 5:16). Engaging in small groups or accountability partnerships is invaluable in sustaining repentance.

3. **Renew your mind**: Transforming habitual sin often starts with renewing thought patterns (Romans 12:2). Memorizing Scripture, meditating on God's promises, and learning to refute lies that lure you into sin are all part of the process.

4. **Practice new habits**: Repentance also involves intentionally replacing sinful habits with godly alternatives. If anger is your struggle, for instance, practice patience and gentleness through intentional acts of kindness and prayerful reflection (Colossians 3:12–14).

Long-term perspective

Turning from past habits can be daunting, especially if you have carried them for years. However, biblical repentance is not a one-time event. It is an ongoing posture of heart, a continual willingness to yield to the Holy Spirit's corrective influence. As you faithfully persevere, you will discover that genuine repentance liberates you from the chains of past behaviors, enabling you to walk increasingly in the freedom Christ provides (Galatians 5:1).

2.2. What is Regeneration?

Repentance, while essential, is only half the story of spiritual transformation. The Bible also teaches the doctrine of regeneration, a miraculous process in which God imparts new spiritual life to the believer. Whereas repentance addresses our turning away from sin, regeneration describes God's supernatural act of granting us a new heart and spirit (Ezekiel 36:26). This profound change occurs beneath the surface of our outward actions, remaking us at the very core of our being so that we become, in the language of Scripture, "new creations" (2 Corinthians 5:17).

2.2.1 The Work of Divine Power

A spiritual rebirth

The term "regeneration" in Titus 3:5 points to "the washing of regeneration and renewal of the Holy Spirit." This highlights that regeneration is not a self-improvement project or a resolution to do better. Rather, it is the Holy Spirit's work, performed in response to one's faith in Christ. Jesus Himself described it to Nicodemus as being "born of the Spirit" (John 3:6). In natural birth, the infant makes no contribution to the process; similarly, in spiritual birth, we rely on God's power to breathe new life into us.

Contrasting with human effort

It is crucial to distinguish regeneration from moral reformation. Moral reformation aims at outward behavior modification, fueled by human determination. While discipline and good habits can momentarily clean up the outside, regeneration transforms the inside first, leading to lasting outward change. You cannot, by willpower alone, produce a truly transformed heart. Only the Spirit of God can replace our heart of stone with a heart of flesh (Ezekiel 36:26). Therefore, regeneration exalts God as the ultimate agent of salvation and underscores our dependence on Him.

Effects on our spiritual senses

When a person is regenerated, their spiritual senses are awakened. Concepts that previously seemed irrelevant—God's holiness, eternity, Scriptural truths—begin to resonate profoundly. Suddenly, the heart hungers for righteousness, the mind becomes open to divine wisdom, and the will inclines to obey God's commandments. This awakening is not merely intellectual; it includes a genuine desire to seek and please God. Regeneration is thus an opening of one's eyes to a spiritual reality previously hidden by sin and spiritual deadness (Ephesians 2:1–2).

A supernatural identity shift

Beyond changing our desires, regeneration brings us into a brand-new identity. Believers are no longer defined by their past sins, failures, or human limitations. Instead, they are children of God, co-heirs with Christ, and temples of the Holy Spirit (Romans 8:16–17; 1 Corinthians 6:19). This identity shift grants the believer not only a future hope but also a present purpose: to live out the reality of the new creation in daily life, bearing witness to God's redemptive power.

2.2.2 The Ongoing Process of Renewal

Understanding progressive sanctification

While regeneration is a decisive event—happening at the moment of salvation—it inaugurates a lifelong process of spiritual growth, often referred to as sanctification. This means that although you are instantly made alive in Christ, the outworking of that new life unfolds over time. Think of regeneration as planting a seed;

sanctification is the gradual development of roots, shoots, and fruit-bearing branches. The seed's nature is fundamentally new from the start, but it needs to grow and mature.

Daily yielding to the Spirit

A believer's cooperation with the Holy Spirit is central to this ongoing renewal. Galatians 5:16 encourages us to "walk by the Spirit" so that we do not gratify the desires of the flesh. This verse indicates that, although we have been regenerated, we must learn to yield daily to the Spirit's direction. Each choice—whether it pertains to relationships, work, entertainment, or personal disciplines—offers an opportunity to grow in grace or slide back into old patterns. Over time, consistent surrender to the Spirit's leading shapes our character increasingly into the likeness of Christ (2 Corinthians 3:18).

Challenges and setbacks

The ongoing nature of renewal can be discouraging when we face personal failures or slow progress. However, setbacks do not nullify the reality of regeneration. Indeed, the capacity to recognize our shortcomings and desire to overcome them is itself evidence of the Holy Spirit at work. As the apostle Paul confessed in Romans 7, even he wrestled with conflicting desires and occasional spiritual defeats. Yet he also found hope in Christ, who empowers us to press on. The presence of the struggle itself can indicate that we are indeed alive to God, longing to live up to our new identity.

The goal: Christlikeness

Scripture presents a lofty vision for the believer: to be conformed to the image of Christ (Romans 8:29). Regeneration is the starting point that makes this conformity possible. Day by day, as we yield to the Holy Spirit, practice spiritual disciplines, and remain anchored in God's Word, the Holy Spirit chisels away at our old nature, revealing the beauty of Christ's character in us. This long-term trajectory reminds us that the Christian life is neither static nor regressive; it is a continuous journey deeper into the heart of God.

2.3. Grace and the New Birth

While repentance and regeneration describe the *what* of our spiritual transformation, grace explains the *why* and *how*. Grace is the divine favor God extends to humanity, making salvation possible despite our unworthiness. Through grace, God offers us forgiveness and new life, not because of our merits, but because of His loving kindness. When we delve into the role of grace in the new birth, we begin to grasp that every stage of our salvation—from conviction of sin to eventual glorification—is rooted in God's lavish benevolence.

2.3.1 Grace Defined and Applied

The biblical concept of grace

In Scripture, grace is often depicted as charis (in Greek), signifying gift, favor, or goodwill. One of the most frequently cited verses on this topic is Ephesians 2:8–9: "For it is by grace you have been saved, through faith—and this is not from yourselves, it is the gift of God—not by works so that no one can boast." This passage plainly teaches that salvation is an unearned gift. We do not initiate it, nor do we sustain it by our own virtue. Rather, grace flows entirely from God's character, revealed supremely in Christ.

A remedy for human inability

The necessity of grace arises from the human inability to save ourselves. Since the fall of Adam and Eve, sin has infiltrated every aspect of our nature (Romans 3:23). We are both guilty of sin and enslaved by it, lacking the capacity to restore fellowship with a holy God on our own terms. Grace, therefore, provides the rescue we cannot achieve. It breaks the chains of guilt and condemnation, offering pardon and power through Christ's atoning work on the cross.

Grace as both an invitation and an empowerment

Grace does more than invite us to salvation; it also empowers us for righteous living. Titus 2:11–12 declares that the grace of God "teaches us to say 'No' to ungodliness and worldly passions, and to live self-controlled, upright and godly lives." This means grace doesn't merely cancel out our past sins; it also teaches and enables us to walk in the newness of life. It is crucial to recognize that grace is not a passive indulgence of our sins but an active force that trains us in godliness.

Avoiding extremes

In discussing grace, we must be careful to avoid two opposite errors. The first is legalism, where individuals try to earn God's favor through strict rule-keeping and moral performance. Legalism drains the joy out of faith and ultimately denies the sufficiency of Christ's sacrifice. The second error is license (or antinomianism), the idea that grace gives us a free pass to sin without consequence. Genuine grace is transformative, not permissive; it beckons us into a lifestyle that reflects God's holiness.

2.3.2 Practical Implications in Daily Living

Security and assurance

When you truly grasp grace, you find security in your relationship with God. Because salvation is not based on your worthiness, you need not live in constant fear of losing God's favor. While unrepentant sin can hinder fellowship with God, it does not destroy the foundation of grace upon which our salvation stands (Romans 8:1). This assurance fosters deep gratitude and worship, motivating us to seek God wholeheartedly.

Humility in interactions

Grace also transforms how we relate to others. Realizing that you have received unmerited favor encourages a humble approach to interpersonal conflicts and judgments. Instead of arrogance, there is a readiness to forgive and a desire to show kindness. Ephesians 4:32 urges believers to be kind and tenderhearted, forgiving one another "as God in Christ forgave you." Understanding that we have been forgiven an incalculable debt paves the way for gracious dealings with others, especially those who have wronged us.

Dependence on God

Practically, living by grace means maintaining a posture of dependence on God. We do not rely on our own intelligence, moral achievements, or natural talents to live the Christian life. Instead, we continually draw upon God's strength, trusting His Spirit to guide us in truth and holiness. Prayer, therefore, becomes a lifeline, not a religious formality. Moments of weakness become opportunities to lean on God's power, as the apostle Paul declared in 2 Corinthians 12:9–10, recognizing that God's grace is sufficient in every trial.

Motivation for service

Finally, grace provides the proper motivation for Christian service.

We do not serve God to earn points or prove ourselves worthy. Rather, service becomes an outflow of gratitude. The apostle Paul's life exemplifies this principle. Once a persecutor of believers, he recognized that God's grace had redeemed him from spiritual ruin (1 Corinthians 15:9–10). This revelation fueled his passion for preaching the gospel and ministering sacrificially. Likewise, when we comprehend the magnitude of God's grace in our own lives, our hearts overflow in love toward God and others, manifesting in joyful acts of service.

2.4. Living Out a Transformed Heart

If repentance and regeneration describe the initial turning to God and the inner change is the direct effects, and if grace is the divine fuel powering that process, then a transformed heart is the ongoing, visible result of these realities in action. Living from this renewed heart is not a temporary phase but the believer's continual calling. It affects our character, relationships, and witness to the world around us.

2.4.1 Consistent Character Change

Spiritual authenticity over superficial change

One hallmark of a truly transformed heart is a consistent reflection of godly character in everyday life. Authentic transformation goes far beyond Sunday church attendance or religious jargon. It penetrates how we handle stress at work, how we speak to family members, and how we respond to moral dilemmas. The apostle John emphasizes that "Whoever says he abides in Him ought to walk in the same way in which He walked" (1 John 2:6). The consistency referred to here is not perfection but a genuine trajectory toward Christlikeness that permeates all areas of life.

Putting off the old self

A crucial biblical metaphor for character change is found in passages like Ephesians 4:22–24, which exhorts believers to "put off your old self" and "put on the new self." The phrase "put off" conveys an active decision to discard sinful behaviors and thought patterns, while "put on" implies an intentional adoption of attitudes and actions consistent with the new nature we have in Christ. This daily routine of putting off and putting on underscores that transformation involves both the negative aspect (rejecting sin) and the positive aspect (embracing righteousness).

Internal motivations and desires

Character change ultimately arises from transformed desires, not just altered conduct. When you are born again, God refocuses your heart's affections. Though temptations still arise, there is a deeper, Spirit-fueled inclination toward holiness. This is why external rule-following never suffices to produce real transformation. We can appear righteous outwardly while our hearts remain self-centered or corrupt. True transformation starts from the inside, aligning our motivations with God's own heart. Psalm 37:4 captures the synergy well: "Delight yourself in the LORD, and he will give you the desires of your heart." This verse does not promise that God fulfills selfish wishes but that He reshapes our desires as we delight in Him.

Ongoing moral vigilance

Even with a regenerated heart, believers must remain vigilant. The remnants of the old nature can resurface if not continually surrendered to God. Regular self-examination, prayer, and community accountability help maintain spiritual growth. Indeed, Scripture presents the Christian journey as a pilgrimage, one where the believer daily chooses to walk in step with the Spirit rather than revert to old habits. It's a dynamic relationship that invites both God's enabling power and our responsive obedience.

2.4.2 Fostering Genuine Relationships

Love as the central ethic

Jesus declared that the greatest commandments are to love God with our entire being and to love our neighbors as ourselves (Mark 12:30–31). Therefore, a transformed heart naturally expresses itself through genuine, Christlike love toward others. The apostle Paul famously expounds on the nature of Christian love in 1 Corinthians 13, depicting it as patient, kind, humble, and selfless. When our hearts are regenerated, we gain both the motivation and the capacity to practice this kind of love—one that transcends mere sentiment and moves toward sacrificial action.

Reconciliation and peace-making

Genuine relationships require vulnerability, forgiveness, and reconciliation—areas in which the transforming power of repentance and regeneration shines. A heart renewed by grace seeks to bridge divides rather than widen them. This can involve apologizing when wrong, extending forgiveness even when it's not requested, and working actively to restore broken trust. Matthew 5:9 pronounces a blessing on peacemakers, indicating that seeking peace is an integral part of kingdom living. Whether the conflict is personal, familial, or communal, believers are called to be agents of reconciliation, modeling how God reconciled us to Himself through Christ (2 Corinthians 5:18–19).

Bearing one another's burdens

A transformed heart recognizes that we are designed for community. Galatians 6:2 implores believers to "Bear one another's burdens, and so fulfill the law of Christ." This means that living out a regenerated life extends beyond personal piety and enters the realm of compassionate involvement in others' lives. Helping a friend through financial difficulty, being present for someone grieving, or mentoring a younger believer are practical ways to demonstrate that your heart—once inclined toward self-interest—now beats in rhythm with God's compassionate heart.

Vulnerability in fellowship

Fostering genuine relationships also involves the willingness to be vulnerable about one's struggles. Often, pride or fear of judgment hinders us from sharing our weaknesses. However, James 5:16 advises believers to "confess your sins to each other and pray for each other so that you may be healed." Such openness deepens relational bonds and allows grace to flow in the community. In a setting where the transformative power of repentance and regeneration is understood, vulnerability is met not with condemnation, but with empathy, prayer, and support.

Conclusion

As you reflect on the truths of this chapter, consider how repentance and regeneration are actively at work in your own life. Are there areas where genuine contrition is needed, perhaps areas long held under the guise of regret but never surrendered? Is the reality of regeneration something you celebrate, or have you fallen into the trap of trying to reform yourself without relying on the Holy Spirit's power? How does the grace of God inform your daily decisions, shaping your view of prayer, worship, service, and relationships?

These questions can lead to profound growth when approached with an open heart. Indeed, repentance is not a one-time checkpoint but a lifelong attitude of turning to God whenever we go astray. Regeneration is not a stagnant status but a living, dynamic process that continually renews us. Grace is not a bare doctrine but a daily gift we can rely upon to sustain us in every circumstance; and transformation is not a distant ideal but an ever-present reality, molding us into the likeness of Christ one day at a time.

May the Holy Spirit guide you to a deeper understanding and application of these life-giving truths. As you move forward, the lessons learned here provide a crucial framework for exploring subsequent chapters in this book. They will underpin discussions of the believer's ongoing growth, the power of the Holy Spirit, the renewal of the mind, and the ultimate call to love and serve others.

Chapter 3: The Power of the Holy Spirit: Transforming from Within

Walking the Christian journey requires more than human wisdom or moral resolve—it calls for divine empowerment. The Bible teaches that this empowerment is provided by the Holy Spirit, often referred to as the "Helper," "Counselor," or "Spirit of Truth." While belief in Christ ushers a person into a relationship with God, it is the Holy Spirit who shapes, strengthens, and guides the believer from the inside out. Many acknowledge the Holy Spirit as part of the Trinity, yet struggle to comprehend His practical role in daily life. This chapter seeks to bridge that gap by emphasizing the Spirit's transformative power, revealing how He indwells believers, empowers spiritual growth, and nurtures visible fruit that testifies to God's redemptive work.

3.1. Understanding the Holy Spirit

Who is the Holy Spirit, and why is His work so central to the Christian life? These questions often arise when believers consider the Spirit's identity. Since the Holy Spirit is spirit—rather than flesh and blood—His activity can be more challenging to grasp than that of Jesus, who walked the earth in human form. Moreover, certain cultural or doctrinal distortions sometimes obscure the Spirit's true nature. Understanding the Holy Spirit begins with recognizing that He is fully God, co-equal with the Father and the Son, yet functioning in a unique role within God's redemptive plan.

3.1.1 His Role in Believers' Lives

The Holy Spirit as a divine Helper

In His farewell discourse, Jesus promised His disciples an abiding presence who would guide them into all truth. Referring to the Holy Spirit, He said, "And I will ask the Father, and he will give you another Helper, to be with you forever" (John 14:16). In the original Greek, the term often translated "Helper" is *Parakletos*, carrying the sense of advocate, counselor, or one who comes alongside. This highlights the Spirit's supportive, nurturing role in our day-to-day walk of faith. He does not merely issue commands from above but dwells with and in believers, offering wisdom and strength as they face the uncertainties and trials of life.

Teacher and guide into truth

The Holy Spirit's role as teacher also comes into focus when Jesus states: "He will teach you all things" (John 14:26). The Spirit reveals spiritual truths that remain opaque to the unbelieving mind. Passages that once seemed cryptic or irrelevant suddenly ring with clarity when the Spirit opens our understanding. The Spirit is not introducing new doctrines that contradict Scripture; rather, He helps us perceive the depth and richness of what God has already spoken. By relying on the Spirit, we avoid errors that can stem from purely human reasoning, thus maintaining alignment with biblical truth.

Conviction of sin and righteousness

Additionally, the Holy Spirit convicts the world of sin, righteousness, and judgment (John 16:8). While this verse applies to the broader world, believers also experience the Spirit's convicting work when they stray from God's path. He pricks our conscience, alerting us to words, thoughts, or deeds that undermine our fellowship with Christ. Far from condemning us, this conviction is a merciful correction, drawing us back to the path of obedience and spiritual health. The Spirit's gentle voice often speaks in moments of moral compromise, prompting us to repent and walk in righteousness.

Intercessor in prayer

Romans 8:26–27 reveals yet another role of the Holy Spirit: helping us in prayer when we are weak or uncertain. "For we do not know what to pray for as we ought, but the Spirit himself intercedes for us with groanings too deep for words." When words fail, the Spirit searches our hearts and conveys needs we cannot articulate. This comforting truth assures us that we are never alone in our communion with the Father; even our wordless sighs and deepest pains are understood and presented before Him by the Spirit's intercession.

Equipper for service

Though we will discuss empowerment in greater depth later, it is worth noting here that the Holy Spirit equips believers for service in God's kingdom. In the Book of Acts, the early church leaders rely on the Spirit for boldness, guidance, and miraculous works (Acts 9:31; 13:2–4). Today, the Spirit continues to impart spiritual gifts— special abilities bestowed for the edification of the church (1 Corinthians 12:4–7). Whether preaching, teaching, encouraging, administering, or showing mercy, these gifts find their source in the Spirit, enabling believers to fulfill God's calling effectively.

3.1.2 Dispelling Common Misconceptions

The Holy Spirit is not an impersonal force

One prevalent misconception is that the Holy Spirit is a mysterious energy or cosmic force rather than a personal being. Scripture, however, attributes personal characteristics to the Spirit: He grieves (Ephesians 4:30), speaks (Acts 13:2), and can be lied to (Acts 5:3). Viewing the Holy Spirit as an "it" rather than a "He" reduces Him to an abstract phenomenon. In contrast, seeing the Spirit as a personal member of the Godhead fosters a richer relationship— one marked by conversation, intimacy, and responsiveness.

He is not limited to charismatic manifestations

Another misconception confines the Spirit's activity solely to spectacular signs such as speaking in tongues, prophecy, or miracles. While the Holy Spirit certainly can and does manifest in miraculous ways, focusing on these phenomena alone can lead to imbalance. The Spirit's work is far broader, encompassing character transformation, the bestowal of spiritual gifts, inner guidance, and more. Restricting the Spirit's influence to flashy experiences risks neglecting His crucial role in everyday growth, ethical choices, and the cultivation of Christlike love.

Emotionalism is not the same as the Spirit's presence

In some circles, the Holy Spirit's movement is equated with emotional exuberance—fervent shouting, dancing, or weeping during worship. While genuine encounters with God can indeed stir strong emotions, not all emotional displays stem from the Spirit. Conversely, a more subdued expression does not imply a lack of Spirit. The Holy Spirit can move powerfully in silent awe, intellectual insight, or quiet conviction just as much as in boisterous celebration. Mistaking heightened emotion for the Spirit's definitive sign can lead to confusion and even spiritual burnout when emotions inevitably wane.

The Spirit does not operate contrary to Scripture

Some believers fear that focusing on the Holy Spirit invites subjective experiences that could undermine biblical authority. But properly understood, the Holy Spirit never operates outside the boundaries of God's revealed Word. Indeed, He is the One who inspired Scripture in the first place (2 Peter 1:21). Any "leading" attributed to the Spirit that contradicts clear biblical teachings must be questioned. By testing spiritual experiences against Scripture, believers remain anchored in God's truth while remaining open to the Spirit's living, active guidance.

Overemphasizing or neglecting

One final misconception arises when Christians swing to extremes—either overemphasizing the Spirit's gifts above all else or almost ignoring His presence. The healthy biblical approach is a balanced reverence, recognizing the Holy Spirit as both the source of supernatural gifts and the One who quietly nurtures our character. When the Spirit is rightly understood as a full person of the Trinity, worthy of worship and fellowship, we neither reduce Him to a means of spiritual excitement nor neglect His daily ministry in our hearts.

3.2. Indwelling and Empowerment

Having established who the Holy Spirit is and dispelling common misconceptions, we now examine two of His core ministries in the believer's life: indwelling and empowerment. The indwelling of the Spirit is an astonishing reality—God choosing to make His home within us. This inward presence then enables the believer to experience power for spiritual growth, service, and perseverance in the face of trials. Together, these aspects highlight that the Christian life was never meant to be lived in isolation from God's enabling presence.

3.2.1 How He Enables Spiritual Growth

God's presence within every believer

Under the new covenant, the Holy Spirit does not merely rest upon individuals temporarily, as occasionally happened in the Old Testament. Instead, He takes up residence within all who put their faith in Christ. Paul describes believers as temples of the Holy Spirit (1 Corinthians 3:16), indicating that God's sanctifying presence dwells intimately in us. This is not a privilege reserved for "super-saints" or church leaders; it is the birthright of every Christian. Once the Spirit indwells the believer, an unbreakable bond is formed, sealing them for redemption (Ephesians 1:13–14).

Shaping character from the inside out

One of the Spirit's primary tasks in dwelling within us is to transform our character into the image of Christ. This process involves renewing our minds, softening our hearts, and reshaping our will. Colossians 3:9–10 describes it as putting off the old self and putting on the new self, which is being renewed in knowledge after the image of its Creator. While that passage does not explicitly mention the Spirit, it nonetheless reflects His inward work of sanctification. Such transformation is often gradual, manifesting in new desires, attitudes, and responses that align with God's righteousness.

Spiritual understanding and discernment

A key element of spiritual growth is discernment—the ability to distinguish truth from error, good from evil, and wisdom from folly. The Holy Spirit grants believers this discernment, enlightening them to the deeper realities of God's Word (1 Corinthians 2:10–14). Even in the midst of cultural confusion or deceptive teachings, the Spirit equips Christians to stand firmly on biblical principles. By immersing ourselves in Scripture and inviting the Spirit's insight, we sharpen our capacity to navigate life's complexities with faithfulness and clarity.

Progressive overcoming of sin

Indwelling by the Spirit also empowers us to overcome sin in a progressive manner. Romans 8:9–14 highlights the contrast between living by the flesh and living by the Spirit, concluding that those led by the Spirit put to death the deeds of the body. This mortification of sin is not a self-willed attempt at moral perfection; it is a cooperative endeavor in which we yield to the Spirit's prompting. As we remain open to His conviction, He reveals areas of compromise or complacency and then provides the strength to resist temptation. Over time, patterns of sin weaken, replaced by godly habits that mirror Christ's own holiness.

Fruitfulness in ministry

Apart from personal transformation, the indwelling Spirit propels believers into fruitful ministry. Even seemingly ordinary acts—like showing hospitality, teaching Sunday school, and praying for a friend—carry divine impact when undertaken under the Spirit's guidance. Ephesians 2:10 teaches that God prepared good works in advance for believers to do, and the Spirit shapes us so we can accomplish them effectively. Thus, spiritual growth is not an inward journey alone; it blossoms outwardly in acts of service that bless the church and the broader community.

3.2.2 The Contrast Between Self-Effort and Spirit-Empowered Living

The limitations of self-effort

One of the greatest traps in the Christian life is attempting to live by self-effort. Even after coming to faith, believers may subtly rely on human strength—disciplining themselves to avoid sin, to read Scripture regularly, or to demonstrate kindness. While discipline has its place, a purely self-reliant approach often leads to frustration, pride when successful, or despair when failing. The apostle Paul lamented this dilemma in passages like Galatians 3:3, asking, "Are you so foolish? Having begun by the Spirit, are you now being perfected by the flesh?" The implied answer is a resounding "no."

Spirit-empowered obedience

In contrast, Spirit-empowered living recognizes that God Himself is the source of our strength, wisdom, and endurance. Zechariah 4:6 famously reminds us, "Not by might, nor by power, but by my Spirit, says the LORD of hosts." When we depend on the Spirit, we approach challenges with a humble awareness of our insufficiency and a confident expectation of God's enabling grace. The outcome is obedience that flows from relationship rather than legalistic duty, fueled by love for God rather than a fear of failure. This dynamic changes how we view everything from worship to conflict resolution: each scenario becomes an opportunity to walk in step with the Spirit, rather than a test of our natural abilities.

Resting in the Spirit's sufficiency

Embracing the Spirit's empowerment also fosters rest. In a world that prizes self-help strategies and personal achievement, believers can find themselves hustling to maintain a spiritual facade. But Jesus offers a different path: "Come to me, all who labor and are heavy laden, and I will give you rest" (Matthew 11:28). While that verse does not explicitly mention the Holy Spirit, it testifies to the rest found in reliance on divine strength. The Holy Spirit becomes the channel of Christ's invitation, enabling us to lay down the burdens of self-made. In this restful posture, spiritual disciplines become life-giving rather than life-draining, as we seek God's presence through the Spirit's leading.

Spiritual warfare and victory

The battlefield of spiritual warfare further illustrates the difference between self-effort and Spirit-empowered living. Ephesians 6:12 states that our true struggle is not against flesh and blood, but against spiritual forces of evil. No amount of human cleverness can conquer these powers. Instead, the believer is called to put on the armor of God (Ephesians 6:13–17), which depends entirely on divine resources—truth, righteousness, faith, salvation, and the Word of God. Praying at all times in the Spirit (Ephesians 6:18) completes the picture, reminding us that victory comes through God's might, not our own. In a war of cosmic proportions, self-effort is both inadequate and dangerous, but Spirit-empowered living assures triumph in Christ.

Freedom from performance-driven faith

When believers grasp the concept of Spirit-empowered living, they find freedom from a performance-driven mentality. Achievements—whether spiritual or otherwise—are no longer measuring rods for self-worth. Instead, success is redefined as *faithful dependence on God*. The soul's motivation shifts from "I must do this to be a good Christian" to "I will do this out of love for God and gratitude for His enabling power." This freedom fosters joy in service, resilience in trials, and deeper intimacy with the God who calls us to abide in Him.

3.3. Signs of a Spirit-Filled Life

The Holy Spirit's transformative presence does not remain hidden. Over time, believers who surrender to His guidance begin to manifest visible signs of a Spirit-filled life. These signs function much like fruit on a healthy tree—evidence that the inner life is vibrant and rooted in divine sustenance. Two key indicators are spiritual fruitfulness and alignment with biblical truth. While there are additional signs we might explore, these two categories offer a starting framework for evaluating whether the Holy Spirit is genuinely at work in a person's life.

3.3.1 Spiritual Fruitfulness

A biblical portrait of the Spirit's fruit

Galatians 5:22–23 provides the classic description of the fruit of the Spirit: "love, joy, peace, patience, kindness, goodness, faithfulness, gentleness, self-control." Each of these virtues serves as a facet of

Christ's character, and their presence signals the Holy Spirit's active influence. Importantly, the passage speaks of *fruit* (singular), indicating an interconnected whole rather than a buffet of separate virtues from which we can pick and choose. As the Spirit works in us, all these qualities grow, albeit at varying rates.

Love: the hallmark of the Spirit

Foremost among these is love (1 Corinthians 13:13). In a Spirit-filled life, love takes on new dimensions—love for God, love for fellow believers, and even love for one's enemies. This love is not merely a sentimental feeling; it is an act of will that seeks the good of others, often at personal cost. Jesus taught that the greatest commandment is to love God wholeheartedly and to love our neighbors as ourselves (Matthew 22:37–39). When the Spirit cultivates love, it transcends natural preferences and moves toward sacrificial compassion, revealing God's own heart to a broken world.

Joy and peace through trials

Another pair of related fruits is joy and peace. Whereas worldly joy relies on pleasant circumstances, Spirit-given joy can flourish in the midst of hardship. Similarly, the peace that arises from the Spirit remains steadfast even when storms of life rage. Philippians 4:7 calls this peace one that "surpasses all understanding," guarding our hearts and minds in Christ. Believers who possess this supernatural tranquility often surprise onlookers who expect panic or despair. Far from naive optimism, this joy and peace is rooted in a deep trust in God's sovereignty and goodness.

Patience, kindness, and goodness

Other facets of the Spirit's fruit revolve around how we treat others. Patience endures offenses without snapping into anger or bitterness. Kindness proactively seeks to bless those around us, sometimes in simple, everyday ways—a gentle word, a helping hand, or an affirming gesture. Goodness, akin to moral excellence, challenges us to reflect God's upright character in a world where ethical compromises are common. Each of these qualities fosters community health, making the body of Christ an inviting place of warmth and genuine care.

Faithfulness, gentleness, and self-control

Rounding out the picture, faithfulness signals reliability and loyalty—qualities that stand in contrast to the fickle commitments of worldly culture. Gentleness suggests a humble disposition, one that neither bulldozes others nor abdicates moral courage but meets people with grace and respect. Finally, self-control points to mastery over impulses and desires. Rather than being governed by whims, the Spirit-filled believer learns to submit each facet of life to Christ's authority, including appetites, emotions, and ambitions. Growing in these areas indicates that the Holy Spirit is steadily remodeling our inner landscape.

3.3.2 Alignment with Biblical Truth

A renewed desire for God's Word

In addition to moral fruit, a Spirit-filled life reveals itself through a growing alignment with biblical truth. When the Holy Spirit works in a believer, He often stirs up a new hunger for Scripture, prompting deeper study and reflection. As 1 Peter 2:2 states, "Like newborn infants, long for the pure spiritual milk, that by it you may grow up into salvation." Such longing transcends intellectual curiosity; it stems from recognizing that God's Word is vital for spiritual nourishment and guidance. Over time, this desire matures into disciplined habits of biblical meditation, enabling the believer to thrive on a steady intake of truth.

Obedience as a response to revelation

The Holy Spirit does not merely give clarity to our understanding of Scripture; He also empowers us to obey what we learn. John 14:21 relates obedience to love for Christ, suggesting that genuine affection for Him manifests in a willingness to keep His commandments. The Spirit fuels this obedience by writing God's laws on our hearts (Hebrews 10:15–16), transforming what might otherwise be a burdensome set of rules into a joyful expression of devotion. When confronted with a scriptural principle that conflicts with worldly norms, a Spirit-led person submits to God's authority rather than capitulating to cultural pressure.

Discernment and theological soundness

Alignment with biblical truth also manifests as theological soundness—a consistent, coherent grasp of the central doctrines of the faith. While not every Christian will possess scholarly expertise, a Spirit-filled believer demonstrates an increasing capacity to discern truth from error. As John 16:13 explains, the Spirit guides believers "into all the truth." Over time, this guidance fosters greater spiritual stability, preventing the believer from chasing fads or succumbing to unbiblical teachings. In an age when misinformation can spread quickly, such discernment proves invaluable for maintaining fidelity to the gospel.

Transformation of thoughts and values

Finally, alignment with Scripture transforms how we think, evaluate, and prioritize. Romans 12:2 exhorts believers to be transformed by the renewing of their minds. The Holy Spirit directs this renewal, helping us cast off worldly mindsets that exalt self, wealth, or power. Instead, He nurtures values that reflect God's kingdom: humility, generosity, integrity, and compassion for the marginalized. This shift in perspective can influence decisions about career, relationships, and daily choices, effectively integrating our faith into every corner of life.

3.4. Practical Steps for Daily Dependence

The Holy Spirit's presence does not operate automatically; believers are invited—and expected—to partner with Him. While salvation is God's gracious gift, living out that salvation calls for ongoing surrender. In this section, we discuss tangible ways to cultivate a day-by-day dependence on the Spirit. Such dependence is not passive laziness; it involves intentional practices that open our hearts to the Spirit's promptings. These practices include prayerful listening, obedience to God's leading, and the cultivation of spiritual sensitivity.

3.4.1 Prayer and Listening

Seeking God in humble petition

Prayer stands at the forefront of Spirit-filled living. Far from a mere ritual, prayer is an interactive dialogue with God, shaped by reverence, honesty, and trust. Believers who wish to rely on the Holy Spirit must consistently bring their needs, desires, and confusions to God, acknowledging their inability to navigate life alone. This humility paves the way for the Spirit to provide wisdom, direction, and comfort. Philippians 4:6–7 promises that when we bring our requests to God with thanksgiving, "the peace of God, which surpasses all understanding, will guard your hearts and your minds in Christ Jesus."

Cultivating stillness and active listening

Yet prayer is not a one-way street of speaking our requests. It also involves listening. In 1 Kings 19:11–12, God spoke to the prophet Elijah not in the wind, earthquake, or fire, but in a gentle whisper. Similarly, the Holy Spirit often communicates in subtle ways— through a thought, a nudge, a heightened awareness of a Scripture passage, or a deep inner conviction. To catch these prompts, believers must practice stillness and reflection. Short, quiet moments throughout the day can become opportunities to check in with the Spirit, asking, "What would You have me do or understand in this situation?"

Discernment in hearing the Spirit

Of course, not every impulse we sense is from the Holy Spirit. Therefore, discernment is essential. We weigh impressions or "inner voices" against Scripture, godly counsel, and the broader witness of the Spirit in our lives. When a potential leading encourages actions or attitudes inconsistent with biblical teaching, we can confidently reject it as a deception or a product of our own desires. Conversely, if it aligns with Scripture's principles, promotes Christlike love, and resonates with mature spiritual counsel, it is likely the Spirit's invitation. Over time, familiarity with God's character sharpens our spiritual hearing.

Persistence and openness

Listening to the Spirit in prayer also requires persistence. The answers may not come instantaneously, nor may they appear in the way we anticipate. Luke 18:1–8 recounts the parable of the persistent widow, illustrating that ongoing prayer can lead to breakthroughs. Being open to God's timing and methods is crucial. Sometimes, the Spirit may guide us through the wise advice of a friend, a sermon, or an unforeseen circumstance. By remaining responsive, we honor the Holy Spirit's sovereignty in orchestrating how He speaks and moves.

3.4.2 Obedience and Sensitivity

Acting on Spirit-given convictions

Dependence on the Holy Spirit is incomplete without obedience. Hearing His voice becomes hollow if we ignore His counsel. James 1:22 warns believers to be doers of the Word, not merely hearers who deceive themselves. When the Holy Spirit reveals a particular sin to forsake, a person to forgive, or a ministry to undertake, we have a decision to make: yield or resist. Spirit-fueled obedience often involves stepping outside our comfort zones, whether that means reaching out to someone in need, confronting an unhealthy habit, or sharing our faith publicly. Yet each step of obedience fosters greater intimacy with the Spirit.

Developing spiritual sensitivity

As we consistently follow the Spirit's guidance, our spiritual sensitivity grows. Much like a musician who hones their ear through practice, a believer learns to recognize the Spirit's voice more clearly over time. Even small acts of faithfulness—speaking a word of encouragement or refraining from gossip—sharpen this sensitivity. Conversely, repeated disobedience or ignoring the Spirit's prompts can dull our perception, making it harder to discern His voice in future situations (1 Thessalonians 5:19 warns against quenching the Spirit).

Guarding against pride and presumption

Growth in spiritual sensitivity can sometimes tempt believers to pride, especially if they see frequent manifestations of God's power or insight. Yet true dependence on the Spirit always deflects glory to God. In 1 Corinthians 1:28–29, Paul reminds us that God chooses the weak and lowly so no one can boast in themselves. The more we experience the Spirit's blessing, the more we should cultivate humility. Recognizing that any gifting, revelation, or fruitfulness stems from God's grace keeps our hearts anchored in grateful worship rather than self-congratulation.

Continual filling and fresh encounters

Ephesians 5:18 exhorts believers to be filled with the Spirit, a command that implies ongoing action. We do not rest on past experiences of the Spirit's presence, but seek fresh infillings daily. This posture ensures we do not stagnate in our spiritual life. Instead, we embrace each new challenge or opportunity as a chance to rely more deeply on the Spirit. Worship gatherings, personal devotions, fellowship with other believers, and even trials can become settings where we invite the Holy Spirit to fill us anew. Such ongoing encounters rekindle our passion and sharpen our capacity to reflect Christ in every aspect of life.

Conclusion

Embracing the Holy Spirit's power moves us beyond the realm of self-effort and religious duty. It anchors us in a dynamic partnership with God, where He shapes our character, equips our service, and fortifies our resolve against spiritual opposition. Far from quenching human initiative, the Holy Spirit rightly channels it, so that our labor in the Lord becomes fruitful and aligned with His redemptive purposes. As we yield to His guidance, we discover that every dimension of life—relationships, decision-making, trials, and triumphs—can become an avenue for encountering God's grace.

Whatever may be the stage of your spiritual journey, the invitation remains the same: seek the Holy Spirit's presence intentionally, submit to His lead consistently, and celebrate the wondrous reality that God Himself resides in you. Each small step of faith, each moment of surrender, and each fresh encounter with His love further cements the truth that God longs to transform you from within—making your life a living witness to His goodness and glory.

Through the power of the Holy Spirit, the Christian life transcends mere human ability, becoming a testimony to the world that God is alive and working in and through His people. May these truths inspire you to open your heart more fully to His transforming presence, fostering a vibrant faith that radiates the beauty of Christ to all you encounter.

Chapter 4: The Renewed Mind: Aligning Thoughts with God's Truth

One of the most overlooked frontiers of spiritual growth is the landscape of the human mind. While much attention is often given to outward behaviors and visible acts of faith, Scripture repeatedly emphasizes that *how* we think profoundly influences *who* we become. A renewed mind does more than simply gather biblical facts or memorize doctrinal statements—it undergoes a deep transformation that shapes every aspect of life, from everyday decision-making to our perception of God, ourselves, and the world around us.

This chapter explores how believers can embrace God's perspective by reorienting their thoughts around His revealed truth. We will begin by examining why the mind matters so greatly, probing the power of thought in spiritual formation and identifying common false narratives that hinder growth. Next, we will delve into the specific processes of mental renewal—replacing old patterns with biblically grounded mindsets and allowing Scripture to guide our beliefs and attitudes. We will then survey practical tools for ongoing transformation, such as reflection, meditation, and the practical application of biblical insights. Finally, we will consider how to cultivate a God-centered perspective through daily disciplines and mutual encouragement within the Christian community. Each of these elements stands as a vital ingredient in developing a thought-life that honors God and fosters spiritual maturity.

4.1. Why the Mind Matters

4.1.1 Power of Thought in Spiritual Formation

Thought as the gateway to transformation

The mind is central to spiritual formation because it shapes the trajectory of our lives. Human behavior does not merely arise out of instinct; it is guided by deeply held beliefs and thought-patterns. Proverbs 4:23 underscores this principle: "Keep your heart with all vigilance, for from it flow the springs of life." While the verse mentions the "heart," in biblical terminology, the heart frequently encompasses our innermost being—thoughts, motives, and affections. Guarding the heart, and by extension, the mind, directly impacts how we live.

The mind's influence on moral and spiritual decisions

People often think of temptation and sin as purely moral or emotional challenges, but the intellectual dimension plays a crucial role. When Eve encountered the serpent in Genesis 3, the tempter did not force her to disobey; rather, he introduced a thought—"Did God really say...?"—that prompted Eve to question God's goodness. This event highlights a fundamental truth: the mind, when influenced by deception, can rationalize or justify actions that stray from God's commands. Conversely, when the mind is anchored in truth, temptation loses much of its power. For this reason, Paul urges believers: "Set your minds on things that are above, not on things that are on earth" (Colossians 3:2).

Transforming the inner narrative

Every individual carries an internal narrative—an ongoing self-talk or commentary about life's circumstances. This narrative weaves together personal experiences, teachings we have absorbed, cultural messages, and assumptions about God or ourselves. If unexamined, such a narrative can block spiritual growth by fostering shame, fear, or false security. On the other hand, when the mind is renewed, the internal story aligns with God's perspective. In Philippians 2:5, believers are exhorted to "have this mind among yourselves, which is yours in Christ Jesus." This statement suggests that we are invited to think as Christ thinks, thereby reshaping the very lens through which we interpret daily life.

Mind and worship

A renewed mind also enriches our worship. While worship involves the heart's affections, it is not detached from intellectual engagement. In John 4:24, Jesus states, "God is spirit, and those who worship him must worship in spirit and truth." True worship arises when our thoughts about God match the reality of who He is—holy, loving, just, and merciful. When the mind is cluttered with distorted ideas about God, worship becomes either hollow ritual or emotional hype. Conversely, as our thoughts align with God's revelation, the mind becomes an avenue for genuine adoration, fueling a worshipful life that extends beyond music into every moment of our existence.

Influence on emotional well-being

The condition of the mind also significantly impacts emotional health. Anxiety, despair, and anger are often rooted in distorted thinking. Scripture offers a remedy: "You keep him in perfect peace whose mind is stayed on you" (Isaiah 26:3). By focusing on God's faithfulness rather than dwelling on worst-case scenarios, the believer finds a stabilizing force for the emotions. This does not mean ignoring painful realities, but rather interpreting life's challenges through the lens of God's truth and promises. Such a mindset fosters resilience, enabling believers to face trials without succumbing to despair.

4.1.2 Battling False Narratives

Identifying deceptive thought-patterns

Every believer must face the reality of spiritual opposition. The enemy's strategy frequently targets the mind with lies that undermine faith and distort God's character. Some common false narratives include:

- **"I am unworthy of God's love."**

- **"God is withholding good from me."**

- **"My past defines my future."**

- **"I must earn God's favor through self-effort."**

While these messages vary in content, they share one goal: to erode the believer's confidence in God's grace and truth.

Recognizing these lies is the first step toward freedom. In 2 Corinthians 10:5, believers are called to "destroy arguments and every lofty opinion raised against the knowledge of God, and take every thought captive to obey Christ." This verse depicts the mind as a battleground where destructive ideologies must be confronted rather than passively tolerated.

Consequences of embracing falsehood

Embracing such false narratives can produce a ripple effect in a Christian's life. For instance, if a person believes they are irredeemably flawed or unworthy, they might shy away from active fellowship, resist serving in ministries, or harbor secret resentment toward God. Over time, this negative self-perception crystallizes into a stronghold, creating emotional and spiritual distance. Another example involves anxiety-driven thinking about the future, which can induce paralysis or constant worry. One's spiritual vitality wanes when fear crowds out trust in God's goodness. Thus, taking every thought captive is not merely an abstract command; it is a matter of spiritual health and maturity.

Unmasking cultural distortions

False narratives not only originate from personal insecurities or spiritual forces; they also arise from cultural norms that conflict with biblical truth. Modern societies often idolize material success, power, or sensual gratification, implicitly suggesting that real worth is tied to wealth or physical attractiveness. Advertising, entertainment, and peer pressure can infiltrate the believer's thinking, clouding what Scripture says about true identity and purpose. When these subtle messages go unchallenged, believers may adopt an incongruent blend of biblical convictions and worldly ambitions. The renewed mind, however, filters cultural values through the standard of God's Word, retaining what is wholesome and rejecting what contradicts divine wisdom (1 Thessalonians 5:21).

Biblical counter-narratives

Overcoming falsehood involves replacing it with truth. The Bible is replete with counter-narratives that uphold God's faithfulness and the believer's identity in Christ. For example, to the lie "I am worthless," Scripture answers: "You are fearfully and wonderfully made" (Psalm 139:14), and "You are God's workmanship" (Ephesians 2:10). To the doubt "God has abandoned me," the Lord promises, "I will never leave you nor forsake you" (Hebrews 13:5). As believers intentionally meditate on these verses, the truth begins to reshape mental patterns, challenging the old scripts that once dictated self-perception or fed chronic fear. This deliberate refocusing of the mind is a key step in spiritual renewal.

4.2. Process of Mental Renewal

4.2.1 Replacing Old Patterns

The scriptural basis for change

The Bible consistently calls believers to undergo a mental transformation. Perhaps the most explicit statement is in Romans 12:2: "Do not conform to the pattern of this world, but be transformed by the renewing of your mind." Here, the apostle Paul sets forth a contrast between passively absorbing worldly influences and actively embracing a God-honoring mindset. The phrase "be transformed" underscores that this renewal is not merely about *adding* new information; it is about internal metamorphosis, akin to a caterpillar becoming a butterfly. The mind is not left to remain as it was—steeped in old habits and assumptions; it is progressively reshaped into something new.

Recognizing the old ways

Replacing old patterns first requires recognizing them. Some harmful mental habits may be so ingrained that they function below the level of conscious awareness. A person might, for instance, operate under a persistent fear of rejection, leading them to either isolate themselves or aggressively seek approval. Another individual might possess a critical spirit, regularly focusing on flaws in others or in their circumstances. Without pausing to identify these patterns, believers might continue in cycles of negativity or self-sabotage. Practically, journaling and introspective prayer can help unearth these hidden thought processes, shining light on areas that require transformation.

Surrender and cooperation

While God initiates renewal, He invites our cooperation. Ephesians 4:22–23 urges believers to "put off your old self... and to be renewed in the spirit of your minds." There is a decisive human action—"put off"—that suggests a willful relinquishing of unhealthy mindsets. Instead of clinging to justifications for bitterness, cynicism, or indulgence, we *submit* these patterns to God. In surrendering them, we make room for the Holy Spirit to implant new attitudes that reflect Christ's character. This collaborative aspect dispels the notion that transformation is entirely passive or solely our responsibility. Rather, it is a divine-human synergy.

Replacing with life-giving truths

Once we recognize and abandon destructive thought patterns, the next step is replacement. Simply repressing or denying negative thoughts often proves ineffective. We need to fill the mental "vacuum" with life-giving truths rooted in Scripture. Philippians 4:8 provides a template for this proactive stance: "Whatever is true, whatever is honorable, whatever is just, whatever is pure... think about these things." Instead of harboring resentment, we cultivate thankfulness; instead of dwelling on failure, we meditate on God's ability to redeem mistakes. Over time, these deliberate choices to affirm what is good and godly reshape our mental default settings.

Ongoing nature of replacement

Crucially, replacing old patterns is not a one-time event. Like an old habit of slouching, negative thinking can resurface unless we remain vigilant. Spiritual setbacks are normal when we have spent years in certain mindsets. The believer must repeatedly realign with truth, catching moments when old narratives sneak in. This iterative process can feel slow, but each small victory builds momentum. Colossians 3:2 commands us to "set your minds on things that are above," implying continual focus. Through perseverance, the new patterns become more natural, and the believer experiences freedom from the cycles that once hindered their relationship with God and others.

4.2.2 Embracing Scriptural Principles

Scripture as the foundation for renewal

The bedrock of mental renewal is God's Word. While popular psychology or motivational materials can offer glimpses of helpful insight, it is ultimately Scripture that provides the authoritative lens on our identity, purpose, and moral compass. Psalm 119:105 portrays God's Word as "a lamp to my feet and a light to my path."

This imagery underscores how Scripture illuminates a believer's journey, safeguarding against pitfalls of ignorance or confusion. By saturating the mind with biblical truth, believers find a reliable anchor amid cultural shifts and personal upheavals.

Guarding against selective reading

To genuinely embrace scriptural principles, however, we must avoid selective reading. It is tempting to focus on passages that affirm our preferences while glossing over those that challenge us. A balanced intake of Scripture—including historical books, wisdom literature, prophetic writings, the Gospels, and the epistles— fosters a holistic view of God and His redemptive plan. Acts 20:27 records Paul's commitment to declaring "the whole counsel of God," suggesting that partial truths can lead to lopsided perspectives. Immersing ourselves in the full breadth of Scripture guards against developing a skewed mindset that clings to comforting themes but ignores the deeper calls to obedience and holiness.

Internalizing biblical truth

Embracing scriptural principles goes beyond intellectual assent; it involves *internalization*. James 1:22 admonishes believers to be doers of the Word, not merely hearers. In practice, this means allowing the Bible's teachings to reshape our moral compass, guide our decisions, and inform our emotional reactions. For example, reading about forgiveness in Matthew 18 leads to evaluating how quickly we release personal grudges. Meditating on Jesus' call to humility in Luke 14 can spark a reexamination of how we handle praise or positions of authority. When Scripture moves from abstract doctrine to lived reality, the mind is renewed, and visible transformation follows.

Personal study and communal engagement

While personal study is crucial, embracing scriptural principles also involves communal engagement. Gathering with fellow believers to discuss and apply Scripture fosters mutual edification. Proverbs 27:17 states, "Iron sharpens iron, and one man sharpens another." Listening to other perspectives, sharing personal insights, and wrestling with difficult passages together enriches our understanding and refines our thought processes. Moreover, Christian community can offer loving correction when someone's interpretation of Scripture strays into error. This corporate dimension ensures that our grasp of biblical truths remains grounded and that the renewing of our minds takes place in the context of nurturing fellowship.

Scripture and cultural engagement

In addition to personal transformation, the renewed mind influences how believers engage with culture. Rather than retreating from societal issues, those who internalize biblical truths can approach topics such as justice, morality, or social responsibility from a well-formed Christian worldview. A mind steeped in Scripture can discern which cultural trends align with God's righteousness and which distort His design. In so doing, the believer not only experiences personal renewal but becomes an agent of renewal in broader societal conversations, providing a reasoned and compassionate voice that points others toward God's redemptive plan.

4.3. Tools for Ongoing Transformation

4.3.1 Reflection and Meditation

Biblical precedent for meditation

Scripture frequently encourages believers to ponder God's Word deeply and deliberately. Psalm 1:1–2 praises the individual who meditates on God's law "day and night," likening that person to a tree planted by streams of water, consistently nourished and fruitful. Meditation, in this biblical sense, entails focused thought on God's character, His works, and His commandments, allowing them to shape one's inner life.

Benefits of reflective practice

Regular times of meditation and reflection yield several benefits:

1. **Deeper understanding**: By dwelling on a passage— examining its context, main themes, and underlying principles—believers move beyond surface-level readings. This can uncover nuances often missed in quick devotions.

2. **Heart-level application**: Reflection creates space to ask how a scriptural truth intersects with personal circumstances. It ensures the text is not merely filed as "information," but allowed to challenge and comfort the heart.

3. **Renewed perspective**: Pausing to meditate can reframe a difficult situation, reminding believers of God's sovereignty or faithfulness. This shift in perspective becomes a bulwark against anxiety or hopelessness.

Methods of meditation

There is no one-size-fits-all approach to biblical meditation; different methods can suit different personalities and seasons of life:

- **Lectio Divina**: An ancient practice of reading Scripture slowly (lectio), reflecting on its meaning (meditatio), praying in response (oratio), and resting in God's presence (contemplatio).

- **Thematic study**: Selecting a biblical theme (e.g., compassion, holiness, wisdom) and meditating on various verses that address it. This allows the mind to see how a concept unfolds across Scripture.

- **Verse-by-verse reflection**: Focusing on a single verse or short passage for a set period, perhaps a week, continually revisiting it to glean deeper insight.

- **Writing and journaling**: Recording insights or prayers in a journal can anchor one's thoughts and provide a record of spiritual growth over time.

Fostering stillness

In a culture saturated with noise and instant communication, cultivating stillness is paramount. Elijah's encounter with God in 1 Kings 19 suggests that God's voice was not in the spectacular wind, earthquake, or fire, but in a "low whisper." Modern life, filled with smartphones and media streams, often drowns out the soft promptings of the Spirit. By setting aside regular intervals for quiet meditation—turning off distractions, breathing deeply, and opening the heart to God—believers can nurture a receptive mindset that is increasingly attuned to divine wisdom.

Overcoming common obstacles

Consistent reflection faces obstacles such as busyness, restlessness, or even mental fatigue. However, small, deliberate steps—a few minutes of silence at the start or end of the day—can begin rewiring the mind. The key is perseverance. Over time, what feels awkward or forced transforms into a cherished spiritual discipline. By combining Scripture reading with reflective prayer, believers anchor themselves in God's promises and develop the focus required for true mental renewal.

4.3.2 Applying Biblical Insights

Knowledge versus application

Biblical knowledge alone does not equate to a renewed mind. James 2:19 starkly observes that even demons *know* truths about God. Genuine transformation requires applying those truths in daily life. To illustrate, understanding the concept of patience intellectually does not make a person patient. Real growth occurs when a believer chooses patience in stressful family dynamics or a challenging work environment—drawing on scriptural guidance in the heat of the moment.

Obedience as an act of trust

When believers apply biblical insights, they express *trust* in God's wisdom. For instance, the Bible's call to forgive those who wrong us can appear counterintuitive or even unjust from a worldly standpoint. However, acting on this command demonstrates belief that God's ways are ultimately life-giving, even if they clash with natural inclinations. In Matthew 7:24–25, Jesus likens those who *do* His words to a wise man building on a rock. When storms come, that firm foundation protects against ruin. So also, in life's trials, the believer who practices scriptural truths stands on stable ground.

Practical "faith experiments"

One helpful way to integrate biblical insights is through faith experiments—deliberate, time-bound practices that test how biblical principles work in real situations. For example, a believer wrestling with worry could commit to practicing Philippians 4:6–7 daily for a week, praying specifically about anxieties and noting the impact on their stress levels. Another might test the principle of generosity in 2 Corinthians 9:6–7 by giving sacrificially for a season and observing how God meets their needs. These experiments shift biblical concepts from abstract ideals to tangible realities, reinforcing the mind's conviction that God's Word is practical and true.

Accountability and guidance

Accountability also strengthens application. Sharing one's plans for implementing biblical insights with a trusted friend or mentor can foster consistency. Proverbs 11:14 affirms the safety found in a multitude of counselors. When a believer articulates how they intend to change thinking patterns or behaviors, it invites external support and feedback. Moreover, a supportive community can celebrate small victories and offer encouragement when challenges arise, thus reinforcing the renewed mindset through shared commitment.

Celebrating incremental progress

Because the process of aligning thoughts with God's truth is gradual, it is essential to celebrate incremental progress. A shift from chronic complaining to occasional gratitude is still progress; a temper that once flared daily might now do so weekly. By noticing and thanking God for these milestones, believers stay motivated.

Such positivity also combats the perfectionist mindset that demands overnight transformation, reminding us that God delights in our steady journey toward Christlikeness.

4.4. Cultivating a God-Centered Perspective

4.4.1 Daily Habits and Disciplines

Establishing rhythms of renewal

A renewed mind thrives on consistent spiritual rhythms—daily patterns that anchor thought-life in God's truth. These rhythms might include morning prayer, evening reflection, scripture memorization, or regularly scheduled fasts. Such disciplines shift our attention away from the clamor of daily demands and back onto God's character and promises. Like training for a sport or learning a musical instrument, mental renewal benefits from structured practice.

Scripture memorization for quick recall

Memorizing Scripture is a potent discipline for mind renewal. Psalm 119:11 notes, "I have stored up your word in my heart, that I might not sin against you." When the truths of God's Word are readily accessible in memory, they can swiftly counter negative thoughts or temptations. For example, in moments of fear, recalling verses that highlight God's protection can diffuse anxiety before it escalates. The discipline of memorization ensures that biblical truths permeate the mind beyond the confines of scheduled devotions, influencing spontaneous thoughts and reactions throughout the day.

Regular times of thanksgiving

Another discipline that cultivates a God-centered perspective is gratitude. A daily practice of enumerating blessings—whether material provisions, relational joys, or spiritual insights—shifts the mind from scarcity to abundance. This alignment with thankfulness stands in stark contrast to worldly messaging, which often stokes discontent and entitlement. First Thessalonians 5:18 instructs believers to "give thanks in all circumstances," suggesting that gratitude is not contingent on perfect conditions but flows from recognizing God's goodness in every season. As gratitude becomes habitual, it softens the mind to embrace and trust God's ongoing work.

Fasting as mental reset

While fasting is traditionally associated with abstaining from food, it can also include stepping back from media or other distractions for a designated period. This temporary denial of physical or mental stimuli creates space to focus on God. In Matthew 6:16–18, Jesus assumes that His followers will fast, implying its place in a robust spiritual life. During such fasts, believers might dedicate extra time to prayer, Scripture study, or worship, allowing the mind to recalibrate. Freed from usual routines, the believer can discern deeper truths and purge mental clutter, paving the way for renewed thoughts.

Journaling and self-examination

Maintaining a journal of thoughts, prayers, and reflections supports a God-centered perspective over time. By reviewing journal entries, believers can trace patterns of growth, identify recurring struggles, and see how God has answered prayers. This discipline fosters self-awareness and encourages honest assessment of where the mind might still cling to falsehood. In

Lamentations 3:40, we read, "Let us test and examine our ways." Journaling brings clarity, capturing fleeting impressions and turning them into tangible records that can guide future decision-making and spiritual direction.

4.4.2 Encouraging One Another Toward Growth

The communal dimension of mind renewal

Though the mind's renewal is deeply personal, Scripture portrays spiritual growth as a communal endeavor. Hebrews 10:24–25 exhorts believers to "stir up one another to love and good works... encouraging one another." Encouragement here encompasses the realm of thoughts and attitudes. A believer can help another recognize mental strongholds or self-defeating narratives, providing loving feedback to steer them back toward biblical truth. This supportive context combats isolation—a prime environment for destructive thinking to fester.

Small groups and discussion circles

Small groups or discussion circles can be fruitful venues for cultivating a God-centered perspective. In a confidential, caring environment, participants can share struggles in their thought-life, explore Scripture collaboratively, and pray for mutual renewal. Such groups might focus on specific themes, like overcoming anxiety or developing confidence in God's promises. James 5:16 affirms the power of confession and prayer in fostering healing, which can include the healing of mental strongholds. By hearing how others apply biblical truths, group members expand their understanding and often discover fresh perspectives on issues they face.

Mentoring and spiritual direction

Mentoring relationships or spiritual direction pairs a more mature believer with one seeking deeper growth. The mentor's role is not to dictate solutions but to listen, ask probing questions, and guide the mentee in discerning God's voice. This personalized approach can unearth mental barriers or patterns that generic teaching might overlook. For instance, a mentor might notice that the mentee repeatedly expresses a sense of unworthiness, gently pointing them to passages affirming God's love (e.g., Zephaniah 3:17, which portrays God rejoicing over His people). Over time, these intentional conversations cultivate a mindset increasingly anchored in gospel truth.

Corporate worship as renewal

Gathering for corporate worship also fosters mental renewal. While worship services often include songs and sermons, they also serve as communal declarations of truth. Singing hymns or worship choruses that proclaim God's character can recalibrate anxious or self-focused thinking. Listening to biblically grounded teaching clarifies doctrines that shape one's worldview. Moreover, testimonies from fellow believers can challenge cynicism or discouragement, reminding the mind that God is at work within the community. Such shared experiences fortify individual convictions and weave them into a collective tapestry of faith.

Extending encouragement beyond church walls

Finally, believers can encourage one another informally throughout the week—through text messages, calls, social media interactions, or spontaneous meet-ups. In these casual contexts, a timely scripture reference or a reminder of God's faithfulness can reorient a friend's troubled mind. Even a brief conversation can plant a seed of hope or conviction. This ongoing network of support exemplifies the essence of the Christian body, where each member contributes to the renewal and flourishing of others (Ephesians 4:16). As individual minds are renewed, the entire community reflects God's character more vividly.

Conclusion

A renewed mind lies at the core of a vibrant Christian walk. Far from being an optional "upgrade" for especially devoted believers, it is an essential facet of discipleship that affects every dimension of life—worship, relationships, emotions, and personal calling. By exploring *why* the mind matters, we have seen that thoughts shape identity and conduct, serving as either gateways to spiritual formation or barriers to growth. We examined the process of identifying and dismantling false narratives, replacing them with biblical truth that fosters wholeness and freedom.

Yet mental renewal does not occur in a vacuum. It requires intentional cooperation with God's revelation and consistent application of scriptural principles. Through disciplines such as reflection, meditation, memorization, and practical faith experiments, believers translate divine truths into lived realities. This journey of transformation involves a daily choice to abandon destructive thought patterns and embrace God's life-giving perspective. As old ways of thinking loosen their grip, the believer experiences increasing clarity, peace, and moral fortitude— tangible evidence that God's Word indeed has the power to transform from within.

Above all, a renewed mind positions believers to fulfill their ultimate purpose: to love God wholeheartedly and love others selflessly. When our thoughts align with God's truth, our worship becomes authentic, our relationships become vessels of grace, and our hearts become eager to serve the kingdom. It is a lifelong process. There will be setbacks, moments when old patterns resurface, or when cultural pressures challenge our convictions. Yet each day offers fresh opportunities to re-engage God's Word, invite the Holy Spirit's guidance, and lean on the fellowship of saints who share the same calling.

May these insights spur you to intentionally guard your thought life, welcoming God's truth to shape your perceptions, guide your decisions, and orient your heart toward genuine worship. In doing so, you will discover that a mindset on God's truth is indeed "life and peace" (Romans 8:6)—a beacon of divine grace shining through your words, your conduct, and your unwavering hope in the promises of the living God.

Chapter 5: The Battle Within: Overcoming the Flesh and Walking in Victory

One of the most challenging realities for Christians to grasp is the ongoing conflict that unfolds within. Even though we have come to faith in Christ, we still wrestle with desires and temptations that do not align with God's will. At times, this struggle can be disheartening: *Why do I still feel drawn to sin if I am genuinely saved?* The New Testament writers acknowledge this tension, describing an inner "battle" between the old nature—often referred to as "the flesh"—and the new, Spirit-led life to which we are called.

This chapter explores the dynamics of that internal conflict, addressing why it persists, how it undermines spiritual vitality, and what believers can do to walk in victory. We will begin by clarifying what "the flesh" means in Scripture and identifying the core aspects of the struggle. Next, we will study practical strategies to overcome this conflict, looking at biblical wisdom that guides us in resisting temptation and cultivating holiness. We will then turn our attention to the believer's spiritual authority—how God equips us to stand firm against the impulses of the flesh and the wiles of the enemy. Finally, we will discuss ways to sustain daily victory through consistent habits, accountability, and a Christ-centered perspective on life.

In confronting this battle within, we must keep in view our ultimate hope: that we are *not* alone in the fight. The Spirit of God empowers us, enabling true transformation and daily triumph over sin's pull. While the struggle is real, the path to victory is equally real—and thoroughly grounded in God's Word and promises.

5.1. Identifying the Struggle

5.1.1 Understanding the Nature of the Flesh

Biblical meanings of 'flesh'

In Scripture, the term "flesh" can carry different shades of meaning. Sometimes it simply denotes the physical body (Genesis 2:23) or humanity in general (Isaiah 40:6). However, in many New Testament passages—especially in Paul's letters—"flesh" points to the fallen, sinful nature that resists the things of God. This usage does not imply the human body is evil in itself but that humanity, post-Fall, is inclined to self-centered desires and rebellion against divine authority.

Paul's teaching in Romans is particularly relevant. He laments that even though he delights in God's law inwardly, there is another principle at work in his bodily members, waging war against the law of his mind (Romans 7:22–23). This "war" is not a casual disagreement but a protracted struggle that frustrates his desire for righteousness. Such is the nature of the flesh: it sets itself in opposition to God's ways, generating conflict within the believer's heart.

A Legacy of the Fall

The presence of this fleshly inclination in believers stems from humanity's fall into sin as recorded in Genesis 3. When Adam and Eve disobeyed God, they forfeited the pristine fellowship that allowed their desires to be perfectly aligned with His will. Consequently, all their descendants inherited a fractured moral compass, prone to corruption. Though believers are spiritually regenerated, the vestiges of this old nature remain, triggering an internal battle whenever we attempt to live out our identity in Christ.

Not merely bodily impulses

It is important to clarify that "flesh" is not limited to cravings of the physical body (like hunger or sexual desire). While these bodily appetites can be corrupted, the flesh also includes mental or emotional impulses—pride, envy, anger, bitterness, or the need for control. These attitudes, though invisible, can be just as potent as overt sins. The flesh essentially seeks self-gratification and self-glorification: it wants to satisfy its urges on its own terms, disregarding God's rightful place as Lord.

A root cause of spiritual stagnation

Unaddressed fleshly desires lead to persistent sin patterns—areas of recurring struggle that hinder spiritual growth. Some believers might feel trapped in cyclical behaviors: lashing out in anger, indulging in lustful thoughts, or harboring resentment that refuses to forgive. Others might cloak their flesh in socially acceptable forms: an addiction to work for self-validation, seeking approval through social media, or using gossip to manage relationships. Regardless of how it manifests, the flesh operates to keep the believer from experiencing the fullness of life in Christ.

5.1.2 Conflicts Between Desire and Spirit

War of two wills

After coming to faith, a believer is sealed with the Holy Spirit (Ephesians 1:13–14). The Spirit imparts a new capacity to love God, desire holiness, and bear spiritual fruit. Yet the old nature—the flesh—still exerts its influence, pulling in the opposite direction. This tension can be felt acutely like being torn between two masters. On one hand, the Christian longs to please God; on the other, he or she may still crave the fleeting pleasures of sin.

Illustration from Galatians

In Galatians 5:17, Paul vividly captures this dynamic: "For the flesh desires what is contrary to the Spirit, and the Spirit what is contrary to the flesh." The Greek term for "desires" in this verse signifies a strong, passionate craving. Thus, the flesh and the Spirit are not politely at odds; they are diametrically opposed forces, each seeking dominance. While the ultimate victory belongs to the Spirit, believers must consciously yield to Him rather than defaulting to the flesh's demands.

Emotional turmoil and self-doubt

This battle can stir emotional turmoil, especially in new believers who assume that conversion should eliminate all inclination toward sin. When they find themselves still tempted, they may question their salvation or label themselves as failures. This guilt can spiral into deeper defeat if not addressed biblically. Realizing that even mature Christians wrestle with the flesh brings reassurance that the conflict itself is not evidence of spiritual ruin. Indeed, the very presence of a struggle often testifies that the Spirit is at work, convicting and guiding the believer toward holiness.

Obstacles to Spiritual Fruit

The conflict between flesh and Spirit is not just an internal phenomenon; it shapes how we treat others and relate to God. Envy, rivalry, and selfish ambition—works of the flesh (Galatians 5:19–21)—splinter church unity and corrode friendships. Meanwhile, a mind controlled by the flesh might resist prayer, Bible study, or service, preferring distractions or self-indulgence. Over time, such habits can stunt spiritual fruitfulness and erode the believer's confidence in God's promises. This is why recognizing the flesh's strategies and actively resisting them is crucial for growth.

Victory is possible

Scripture never suggests that believers are doomed to perpetual defeat at the hands of the flesh. While the old nature cannot be eradicated in this life, it can be dethroned. As we embrace God's prescribed strategies and walk in the power of His Spirit, the gravitational pull of the flesh loses its hold. This does not mean an absence of temptation, but rather an increasing capacity to say "no" to sin and "yes" to righteousness, reflecting Christ's victory in our daily conduct.

5.2. Strategies for Overcoming

5.2.1 Recognizing Temptations

Definition of temptation

Temptation refers to any enticement or lure to sin. It capitalizes on legitimate needs or desires—food, intimacy, security, success—but twists them toward disobedience or excess. Temptation can arise from external sources, such as worldly messages or peer pressure, and from internal inclinations, such as lust or pride. Understanding how temptations operate is a foundational step in resisting them.

Rooted in deception

At the core of temptation is a deception: the lie that sinful gratification is more fulfilling or necessary than obeying God. In James 1:14–15, we learn that each person is tempted when lured by their own desire. Once the mind entertains that desire, it can conceive sin, leading to destructive outcomes. Because temptation often disguises itself as harmless or beneficial, believers must remain vigilant. The flesh, left unchecked, readily justifies sinful thoughts or actions under the guise of "deserving happiness" or "just this once."

Recognizing personal triggers

One practical step in overcoming temptation is identifying personal triggers—situations, emotional states, or relationships that intensify vulnerability. For instance, some people are more prone to anger when fatigued; others slip into envy when browsing social media. By mapping these triggers, believers can develop proactive responses instead of merely reacting in the moment. This might mean setting healthy boundaries, avoiding certain environments, or learning new coping strategies for stress. Knowing your patterns allows you to circumvent unnecessary battles.

Jesus as a model of resistance

Jesus' own experience with temptation (Matthew 4:1–11) offers valuable lessons. The devil's challenges targeted legitimate desires—hunger, protection, and authority—and twisted them to undermine Jesus' reliance on the Father. Each time, Jesus countered with Scripture, reaffirming God's truth rather than engaging with the lie. This demonstrates the importance of having God's Word accessible in one's mind and heart. When temptation beckons, referencing biblical truths can cut through the illusion that sin is beneficial or unavoidable.

Fleeing vs. fighting

Sometimes, the Bible instructs believers to stand firm against the devil (James 4:7), while at other times it advises fleeing (2 Timothy 2:22). Which approach is correct? Both, depending on the situation. When faced with spiritual opposition that threatens to sway your commitment to Christ's lordship, you resist. But if a specific temptation (e.g., sexual immorality or addictive behavior) consistently exploits your weakness, you may need to flee— physically removing yourself from the environment. Recognizing which stance is appropriate requires discernment. Both resisting and fleeing honor God if done with humility and a reliance on His Word.

5.2.2 Guarding the Heart and Mind

The gatekeepers of action

Scripture emphasizes the heart and mind as the gatekeepers of spiritual health. They filter ideas, shape desires, and determine how external stimuli are interpreted. If a believer neglects vigilance over their internal life, the flesh gains an easy foothold. Hence, Proverbs

4:23 cautions, "Keep your heart with all vigilance, for from it flow the springs of life." "Heart" here merges intellect, will, and emotion. Guarding it means carefully evaluating what we allow to influence our thoughts and affections.

Filtering inputs

In a digital age, believers are bombarded with content—movies, social media, news outlets—much of which glamorizes values contrary to God's Word. Constant exposure to such messages can subtly normalize selfishness or immorality, undermining spiritual alertness. Guarding the heart therefore involves curating our media consumption, mindful of how it shapes our worldview. Philippians 4:8 underscores the importance of directing our minds toward things that are "true... honorable... just... pure... commendable." By choosing wholesome, God-honoring content, we fortify the mind against the flesh's enticements.

Cultivating holy desires

Guarding the heart is not merely defensive. It also involves cultivating holy desires that crowd out sinful ones. For instance, regularly rehearsing God's promises in Scripture can awaken a deeper yearning for righteousness. Serving others in practical ways can kindle compassion that displaces self-absorption. Engaging in sincere worship draws the soul to God's beauty, minimizing the allure of fleeting indulgences. Over time, as these positive practices become habitual, the flesh finds fewer chinks in the believer's armor.

Renewal of the mind

Closely tied to guarding the heart is the **renewal of the mind**, a process highlighted in Romans 12:2, which speaks of being transformed by a new way of thinking. While the detailed discussion of mind renewal is in the previous chapter, it suffices to say that consistent intake of Scripture—through study, memorization, and meditation—reshapes our outlook. The believer increasingly sees life from God's vantage point, making worldly temptations appear shallow and destructive by comparison.

Practical boundaries and wise planning

On a more concrete level, guarding the heart and mind often involves setting boundaries and planning wisely. If late-night internet browsing leads to temptation, it might mean imposing digital limits. If certain friendships consistently pull you toward negative or unwholesome behaviors, you may need to redefine those relationships. Boundaries are not about legalism but about stewarding one's spiritual well-being. A wise believer recognizes vulnerabilities and acts preemptively, trusting that sacrifice in these areas reaps freedom and joy in the long run.

5.3. Walking in Spiritual Authority

5.3.1 Standing Firm in Faith

Believer's authority in Christ

A crucial aspect of overcoming the flesh is recognizing that believers have authority in Christ. This authority does not derive from personal strength or moral superiority but from our union with Jesus, who has defeated the powers of darkness (Colossians 2:15). While the flesh clamors for dominion within us, our position in Christ grants us the right—and the responsibility—to refuse its tyranny. Through faith, we assert that we belong to God, body, and soul, and that sin no longer has legal claim over us (Romans 6:14).

Faith as a decisive stance

Walking in spiritual authority requires faith that God's Word is true and operative. For instance, if God declares that sin's power is broken, we choose to believe this, even when temptation feels overpowering. Ephesians 6:16 describes faith as a "shield" that can extinguish the flaming arrows of the evil one. In the context of the flesh, these arrows may be accusations of unworthiness, reminders of past failures, or strong impulses that suggest victory is impossible. The shield of faith counters these attacks by standing firm on God's promises: we are no longer slaves to sin, but children of the Most High.

Illustration from Israel's conquest

The conquest narratives of the Old Testament often serve as analogies for spiritual battles. In the Book of Joshua, God promised Israel the land of Canaan, but they still had to fight. While God assured victory, each tribe had to step onto the battlefield, trusting God's presence and power. In a similar way, believers today are "more than conquerors" (Romans 8:37), yet we must engage the battle with faith. We do not passively await holiness; we actively contend for it, relying on God's strength.

Declaring truth over emotions

Exercising spiritual authority sometimes involves declaring biblical truth over contrary emotions. When the flesh urges self-indulgence or fosters despair, the believer speaks God's truth into the situation: *I am redeemed; I am empowered by the Spirit; Christ lives in me; I am a new creation.* Such affirmations are not empty mantras but proclamations of a spiritual reality rooted in Scripture. By aligning our words with God's perspective, we fortify the mind against the lies that fuel fleshly desires.

Humility and dependence

Paradoxically, walking in spiritual authority also demands humility. We do not overcome by prideful self-reliance but by depending on God's provision. In 2 Corinthians 12:9, the Lord tells Paul that His power is made perfect in weakness. When confronting the flesh, believers must regularly confess their limitations and ask for divine help. This posture of humility ensures that we do not become self-righteous or harsh toward others struggling with sin. Instead, we operate from a place of gratitude for God's sustaining grace.

5.3.2 Resisting, Renewing, and Rejoicing

A threefold approach

Believers can conceptualize walking in spiritual authority through a threefold approach: resist, renew, and rejoice.

1. **Resist:** Actively oppose the cravings of the flesh, whether by fleeing temptation or standing firm in the armor of God. This resistance is not passive but proactive—identifying weak points, seeking accountability, and praying for deliverance from areas of entrenched sin.

2. **Renew:** Continuously refresh the heart and mind with scriptural truth, prayer, and fellowship. This renewal keeps the spiritual perspective clear, warding off the cynicism or complacency that can arise when struggles persist.

3. **Rejoice:** Remember to celebrate the victories—small or large—that God grants along the way. Rejoicing fosters

hope, reminding us that the process of sanctification is ultimately undergirded by God's steadfast love.

Overcoming condemnation

One of the flesh's tactics is to exacerbate guilt, leading believers to condemn themselves harshly for their failures. This self-condemnation can sap spiritual vitality, making it harder to resist future temptations. By contrast, biblical conviction leads to repentance and restoration, not hopeless shame. Romans 8:1 declares that there is no condemnation for those in Christ Jesus. When believers embrace this assurance, they find the courage to keep fighting the battle within, rather than succumbing to despair.

Persistence in spiritual disciplines

Resisting, renewing, and rejoicing all hinge on consistency in the basic spiritual disciplines: prayer, Scripture study, worship, and fellowship. Sporadic engagement with these disciplines can leave the believer vulnerable, much like a neglected shield or a sword left to rust. But a steadfast routine—daily moments of prayer, weekly fellowship, ongoing reflection on the Bible—ensures a steady supply of spiritual strength. By maintaining these habits even when they feel mundane, believers cultivate resilience against the flesh's attempts to undermine devotion.

The role of praise

In the face of intense temptation or discouragement, praise can be a powerful weapon. Singing or speaking words of adoration shifts focus from the flesh's pull to God's greatness. Biblical examples abound, such as when Jehoshaphat's army led with worshipers, celebrating God's majesty before a great battle (2 Chronicles 20:21–22). Though the context differs, the principle remains:

praising God fosters faith, lifts the spirit, and reminds us that we fight from a position of His victory. In personal battles against sin, intentionally pausing to worship can disrupt negative thought spirals, reminding the believer of God's sovereignty and compassion.

Testimonies of God's deliverance

Hearing or sharing testimonies of God's deliverance from the flesh can also strengthen resolve. When another believer describes their journey from bondage to freedom—whether from addictions, habitual anger, or patterns of deceit—it sparks hope in those who are still struggling. These accounts affirm that the same power that worked in biblical heroes and modern-day saints is available to us. Rather than idealizing the struggle, testimonies highlight God's redemptive grace, illustrating that no fleshly stronghold is too entrenched for Him to overcome.

5.4. Sustaining Daily Victory

5.4.1 Accountability and Community Support

Why isolation fosters defeat

The flesh thrives in secrecy and isolation. When a believer withdraws from accountable relationships, negative habits can flourish unchecked. In solitude, it is easier to rationalize wrongdoing or suppress conviction. Conversely, when we live in open, honest fellowship, the influence of the flesh is brought into the light. James 5:16 instructs believers to "confess your sins to one another and pray for one another," linking confession to healing. While this verse does not refer exclusively to physical healing, it certainly encompasses spiritual and emotional well-being.

Choosing the right confidants

Not everyone can serve as an effective accountability partner. Trust, respect, and spiritual maturity are essential traits in someone with whom you share vulnerabilities. Such a person should be grounded in Scripture, compassionate yet firm, and committed to confidentiality. The goal is mutual edification, not gossip or judgmental scrutiny. When healthy accountability is in place, the flesh finds fewer places to hide. Frequent check-ins or purposeful questions can dismantle patterns of deception that would otherwise persist.

Small groups and mentoring

Community support can also emerge through small groups or mentoring relationships. Meeting regularly with a group of believers who study the Word, discuss personal challenges, and pray for one another builds resilience against fleshly temptations. In such gatherings, members sharpen each other's convictions and bear one another's burdens (Galatians 6:2). Mentoring offers a more focused dynamic: a mature believer invests time in guiding a younger Christian, offering wisdom to navigate specific trials. Both formats cultivate transparency and spiritual growth.

Practical accountability structures

Implementing practical accountability might include sharing personal struggles, setting goals for spiritual disciplines, or installing monitoring software to prevent access to unwholesome content online. It could involve weekly or biweekly calls where each individual honestly reports victories, setbacks, and pressing temptations. Such measures are not about legalistic control but about extending a supportive hand of grace. By acknowledging that the flesh can deceive even the sincere Christian, we take proactive steps to safeguard each other's walk with Christ.

Overcoming shame

One key hurdle in seeking accountability is shame. The flesh loves to whisper that others will judge or reject us if they know our true struggles. But the biblical community counters shame with understanding and compassion. 1 John 1:7 promises that if we walk in the light, we have fellowship and cleansing. Openness about our battles fosters genuine fellowship where hearts can be healed. By stepping into the light, we discover that many believers have faced similar struggles and have found grace sufficient to overcome them.

5.4.2 Developing Spirit-Led Resilience

Daily reliance on God's strength

Even with accountability and disciplined habits, believers must consistently rely on the Holy Spirit's empowerment to sustain victory. This reliance is not passive fatalism; it is an active, moment-by-moment dependence. Ephesians 6:10 admonishes, "be strong in the Lord and in the strength of his might." The idea is to draw on divine resources, particularly when circumstances or inner emotions threaten to derail us. Routine prayers—whether short "breath prayers" during the day or more extended devotions—center our perspective on God's sufficiency rather than our inadequacy.

Perseverance through setbacks

Inevitably, the journey to overcoming the flesh includes missteps. Believers may experience relapses into old patterns or succumb to temptations thought conquered. Such failures can trigger discouragement or condemnation. Yet Scripture provides examples of godly men and women who stumbled but found restoration—David after his sin with Bathsheba, and Peter after denying Christ. In each case, genuine repentance led to renewed purpose. Spirit-led resilience allows believers to learn from failures, recalibrate, and press on in hope. Rather than wallowing in self-pity, we cling to the knowledge that God's grace is abundant and that He works redemptively through our brokenness.

Mindful stewardship of the body

An often overlooked facet of sustaining victory is physical self-care—adequate rest, proper nutrition, and regular exercise. Fatigue or chronic stress can lower resistance to temptation, intensifying the voice of the flesh. Jesus Himself, though perfect, demonstrated the importance of rest and retreat (Mark 6:31). When believers neglect their physical well-being, they risk a compromised mental and emotional state that is more susceptible to sinful impulses. Treating our bodies as temples (1 Corinthians 6:19) not only honors God but also strengthens our capacity to face spiritual battles with clarity.

Cultivating holy habits

Developing resilience also involves cultivating holy habits that reinforce spiritual momentum. For example, regularly practicing gratitude can neutralize envy or dissatisfaction. Scheduling time to reflect on God's blessings shifts focus away from what the flesh claims we lack. Acts of service—helping the poor, volunteering in ministry, or mentoring younger believers—further draw us out of self-centeredness. These habits, repeated over months and years, reshape instincts and diminish the foothold of the flesh. Eventually, generosity, kindness, and humility begin to flow more naturally from a life anchored in Christ.

Long-term vision

Believers who maintain victory over the flesh often share one trait in common: a long-term vision of growth and sanctification. They do not demand overnight perfection but pursue steady progress, trusting that God is continually forming them into the image of His Son (Romans 8:29). This perspective counters the impatience that arises when temptations persist or spiritual breakthroughs seem delayed. By keeping eternal realities in view, we learn to value gradual change and rejoice in incremental victories, confident that the final triumph over sin awaits us in eternity (Revelation 21:4).

Conclusion

The battle within—the conflict between the flesh and the Spirit—is an inescapable reality for every follower of Christ. Yet it need not define us. Scripture not only acknowledges this struggle but equips us with the wisdom and power to walk in victory. By recognizing the nature of the flesh and understanding how it infiltrates our desires, we demystify the source of our struggles. We then adopt strategies grounded in biblical truth—identifying and resisting temptation, guarding our hearts, standing firm in spiritual authority, and celebrating the incremental progress that comes through consistent reliance on God.

Key to this entire journey is the knowledge that the Holy Spirit dwells within believers, providing both the impetus and the strength to say "no" to sin and "yes" to righteousness. Daily victory over the flesh is not a pipe dream or a reward for a select few "super-saints." Rather, it is a promise for all who yield to God's leading, persevere in faith, and nurture accountable relationships within the body of Christ. While stumbles may occur, genuine repentance and renewal are always within reach. God, who began a good work in us, is faithful to bring it to completion (Philippians 1:6).

As you reflect on the battle within, remember that you do not fight alone. Brothers and sisters in Christ stand alongside you, and the Spirit of God upholds you with divine resources. By embracing biblical counsel and daily surrendering your will to the Lord, you can conquer the pull of the flesh and experience the abundant life Jesus promised (John 10:10). Each day of obedience is a day nearer to the full consummation of Christ's victory—a day when the struggle will cease, and we will stand faultless in His presence. Until then, press on, soldier of Christ, for the One who calls you is faithful, and He will equip you to overcome.

By integrating these principles into your walk of faith, you will discover that victory over the flesh is not only possible—it is part of God's gracious plan for your sanctification. Each decision to resist temptation, each moment of surrender, and each step in accountability paves the way for deeper freedom and joy. Indeed, the One who indwells you is greater than the impulses that once held you captive, ensuring that *you can* walk in daily triumph through the power of His Spirit.

Chapter 6: Eternal Perspective: Pressing Toward the Ultimate Prize

At the heart of the Christian journey lies a divine promise that transcends the fleeting realities of this world: the certainty of eternal life with God. Throughout Scripture, believers are encouraged to lift their eyes from immediate trials and fleeting pleasures to behold an everlasting inheritance. This *eternal perspective* is not a form of escapism, but rather a transformative outlook that reshapes priorities, reinvigorates hope, and clarifies the reason behind every sacrifice made in Jesus' name.

Yet cultivating an eternal focus can be challenging in a world filled with distractions. Societal norms often encourage instant gratification, measuring success by wealth, power, or personal achievement. Followers of Christ, however, are called to a different standard, one that looks beyond the next few decades and into the boundless future God has prepared. The tension between living responsibly in the present and awaiting the fullness of God's kingdom generates one of the most dynamic aspects of Christian discipleship.

In this chapter, we will explore the practical outworking of an eternal perspective. We begin by examining how *shifting focus to eternity* fuels a believer's faith, addressing why hope in the life to come is so critical for spiritual stability. Then we consider the *motivation* that flows from this perspective, including the cultivation of godly purpose and the setting of Christ-centered goals. In the next section, we delve into the active dimensions of *pressing on in faith*, especially in the midst of trials and the call to consistent devotion. Finally, we discuss the corporate dimension of encouraging others on the same journey, recognizing that we do not walk alone but are part of a community spurring one another forward. Through it all, we will see how focusing on our eternal inheritance transforms how we work, worship, serve, and endure.

6.1. Shifting Focus to Eternity

6.1.1 The Significance of Eternal Hope

A hope rooted in God's promise

The New Testament resounds with declarations about the believer's future inheritance. The Apostle Peter, for example, exalts God for giving believers a "living hope" through the resurrection of Jesus Christ, describing an incorruptible and undefiled inheritance kept in heaven (1 Peter 1:3–4). This verse underscores that *eternal hope* is not wishful thinking but a solid assurance, founded on Christ's finished work. This promise is more certain than human contracts or financial investments, for it is guaranteed by God's unchanging character.

Why hope matters

Hope plays a vital role in the believer's resilience. Without a clear vision of eternal reward, the Christian life can devolve into a series of rules or moral obligations disconnected from any larger narrative. Robust anticipation of eternity, however, infuses daily choices with meaning. It undergirds sacrificial acts of love, emboldens believers to stand for truth despite opposition, and consoles hearts in times of grief or disappointment. It is a navigational compass, preventing the soul from losing direction amid life's tempests.

Hope as an anchor for the soul

Hebrews 6:19 characterizes hope as "a sure and steadfast anchor of the soul." When storms of doubt or persecution loom, hope stabilizes the believer, keeping faith from drifting into cynicism or despair. Significantly, this hope is not self-generated but anchored *in God Himself*. Throughout the Bible, He reveals a pattern: God's people, though beset by trials, can look ahead with confidence, for He is faithful to fulfill His promises in His perfect timing. One sees this in the narratives of Abraham awaiting Isaac, or Israel longing for deliverance in Egypt. In each case, divine promise, rather than immediate evidence, upheld them.

Contemporary relevance of eternal hope

In modern society, the daily news cycle brims with conflicts, economic uncertainties, and moral confusion. Against this backdrop, an eternal perspective offers a distinctly Christian form of hope that neither denies harsh realities nor is crushed by them. Rather, believers learn to see worldly systems as transient, measuring success and security not by current events but by the larger scope of God's redemptive plan. Such hope fosters peace of mind, as the believer rests in the knowledge that ultimate justice and restoration await.

6.1.2 Viewing Present Circumstances Through a Future Lens

A life reinterpreted by eternity

Cultivating eternal vision means reevaluating the significance of daily events in light of their eternal outcomes. Rather than seeing routine tasks as mundane, the believer discerns eternal implications in seemingly small acts of faithfulness. This approach resonates with Jesus' teaching that even giving a cup of cold water to a disciple has lasting significance (Matthew 10:42). A mother raising her children in the fear of the Lord recognizes that she is shaping eternal souls. A believer quietly interceding for persecuted churches worldwide trusts that prayer ascends before God's throne with eternal impact.

Temporal adversity vs. eternal glory

Paul's letters reflect a recurrent theme of comparing present suffering to future glory. In 2 Corinthians 4:17–18, he writes of "this light momentary affliction" producing an "eternal weight of glory beyond all comparison." Although Paul endured beatings, imprisonments, and many hardships, he perceived these trials as fleeting in comparison to the grandeur of what awaited. Such a perspective does not trivialize pain but places it within a broader redemptive story. Illness, betrayal, or financial loss—while devastating at the moment—gain a different dimension when weighed against the everlasting joy that the believer will share with Christ.

Stewardship of time

A future-oriented mindset shapes how we manage our time. The psalmist pleads, "So teach us to number our days that we may get a heart of wisdom" (Psalm 90:12). When we remember life's brevity and eternity's enormity, our priorities shift. Leisure and rest remain important, but mindless entertainment loses some of its charm as we become more discerning. We ask: *Is this pursuit contributing to God's kingdom or merely squandering resources?* The objective is not frantic busyness but intentional stewardship—choosing tasks and relationships aligned with eternal values.

Reading God's providential fingerprints

Viewing present circumstances through an eternal lens also fosters sensitivity to God's providential guidance. Believers begin to see that no encounter is random, and no moment is wasted if surrendered to God's purpose. A chance meeting at a coffee shop could be an opportunity for a gospel witness. A job setback might be God's way of redirecting us toward a more fruitful path. Though we cannot always interpret events with perfect clarity, an eternal perspective reminds us that God orchestrates even painful detours for His redemptive ends (Romans 8:28). The Christian thus lives expectantly, attuned to the Spirit's nudges in seemingly ordinary spaces.

6.2. Motivation for the Believer

6.2.1 Living with Purpose

From drifting to intentionality

Many people drift through life without a sense of overarching purpose. They choose vocations, relationships, or lifestyles more by chance or social pressure than by conviction. In contrast, an eternal perspective galvanizes believers to live intentionally. Recognizing that God has placed each person on earth to fulfill unique callings, they seek to discover how their gifts, passions, and circumstances can intersect with God's mission. This approach transforms daily routines into meaningful service, whether in a corporate office, a classroom, or a household.

The example of biblical figures

Scripture offers numerous models of purpose-driven living. Nehemiah, for instance, was a cupbearer to a foreign king, but he recognized that God had positioned him to rebuild Jerusalem's walls (Nehemiah 2:5). Esther, an orphan turned queen, risked her life to save her people, famously declaring, "If I perish, I perish" (Esther 4:16). Though their contexts differ, these individuals share a willingness to align their personal roles with God's redemptive plan. When believers adopt a similar posture, they move from passivity to proactive engagement with the world's needs—be it evangelistic outreach, social justice, or mercy ministries.

Integrity and vocational calling

Part of living with purpose involves **vocational integrity**—doing our jobs as unto the Lord. Colossians 3:23 teaches, "Whatever you do, work heartily, as for the Lord and not for men." Viewing one's occupation in light of eternity breaks the artificial divide between "sacred" and "secular." Whether you're a mechanic, writer, healthcare professional, or stay-at-home parent, your labor has eternal reverberations if pursued in faith and excellence. The key lies in recognizing that God cares not only about church-related tasks but also about how we treat clients, the quality of our work, and our testimony to colleagues. The eternal perspective invests in everyday duties with the significance of the kingdom.

Understanding spiritual gifts and passion

Finding purposeful living also involves discerning personal spiritual gifts and God-given passions. Romans 12:6–8 enumerates gifts such as teaching, generosity, leadership, and mercy—abilities entrusted to individuals for the common good of the body of Christ. Similarly, each believer has unique passions or burdens, be it for youth mentorship, global missions, or creative arts. Combining these gifts and passions with an eternal perspective yields potent ministry. Instead of envying others' callings, we realize the body's diverse parts are interdependent, each fulfilling a distinct function to glorify God and serve humanity.

Perseverance through setbacks

Purposeful living is not without obstacles. Failures, rejections, or confusion about one's path can sap motivation. Yet an eternal lens reminds believers that God can reroute missteps for greater fruitfulness. When faced with professional layoffs, ministry conflicts, or health challenges, the Christian does not conclude that all is lost. Rather, they reaffirm that their identity lies in Christ, not in temporal roles and that each trial can refine character for a higher purpose (1 Peter 1:6–7). This resilience flows from the knowledge that God, who assigns callings, also equips and sustains us until the finish line.

6.2.2 Maintaining Christ-Centered Goals

Goals shaped by the gospel

In the Christian context, however, goals are *Christ-centered*—aligned with kingdom priorities and reflecting the humility of the

105

gospel. Instead of striving solely for personal comfort or acclaim, believers aim to love God wholeheartedly, love neighbors sacrificially, and advance the good news of salvation in Jesus. Such goals might include learning to forgive an estranged family member, organizing an evangelistic event, or saving money to support mission work. The overarching aim is to reflect Christ's character and commission, not inflate personal ego.

Balancing ambition with surrender

Healthy ambition, when directed toward God's glory, can be an asset. Paul's zeal to preach Christ where He was not yet known (Romans 15:20) exemplifies righteous ambition. Yet ambition must be tempered by surrender. James 4:13–15 cautions believers against making dogmatic plans independent of God's will. True success requires holding goals loosely, acknowledging divine sovereignty: "If the Lord wills, we will live and do this or that." This posture protects us from anxiety and arrogance. We work diligently, but we also entrust outcomes to God, trusting that He may redirect our plans for higher purposes.

Progress over perfection

Setting Christ-centered goals requires patience and a focus on progress rather than perfection. Sanctification is an ongoing journey; believers often have to reevaluate and adjust their objectives. For instance, an ambitious plan to read the entire Bible in three months might give way to a sustainable approach of meditating on fewer passages deeply. Or a goal to disciple a dozen new converts might be refined to mentoring two or three thoroughly. By celebrating incremental steps, believers keep discouragement at bay. The joy lies in obeying God incrementally, trusting that small acts of faithfulness cumulatively bear eternal fruit.

Evaluating worldly success

While biblical goals can incorporate career growth or financial stability, these must be weighed against the measure of eternal worth. Jesus challenges, "What does it profit a man to gain the whole world and forfeit his soul?" (Mark 8:36). A large salary or impressive title can be blessings if used for kingdom purposes—but they can also become idols. Believers regularly ask: *Does this goal cultivate Christlikeness and serve God's kingdom, or does it merely serve me?* By filtering ambitions through biblical values, Christians avoid hollow successes that may sparkle briefly but have no lasting significance.

6.3. Pressing On in Faith

6.3.1 Perseverance in Trials

Trials as a refining fire

Scripture consistently portrays trials as catalysts for spiritual growth rather than mere obstacles. James 1:2–4 famously exhorts believers to "count it all joy...when you meet trials of various kinds," explaining that testing produces steadfastness. An eternal perspective transforms how we approach pain, loss, or prolonged waiting. Rather than viewing afflictions as signs of divine abandonment, we perceive them as arenas in which God shapes our character, forging qualities such as patience, empathy, and deep trust in His promises.

Historical and global examples

Perseverance in trials is not an abstract concept but a lived reality for millions of believers across centuries. The early Christians faced sporadic but intense persecutions under the Roman Empire, often forced to hide in catacombs or risk execution. Yet their unwavering commitment ultimately bore fruit in the widespread acceptance of the gospel. In modern times, believers in regions hostile to Christianity endure marginalization, imprisonment, or worse. Their tenacity, grounded in the certainty of eternal life, testifies to the power of a future-focused faith. While not all believers face overt persecution, everyday struggles—chronic illness, relational strife, economic hardship—become sanctified challenges when viewed through the lens of eternity.

Prayer and lament

Pressing on in the midst of suffering includes learning to lament. Contrary to stoicism or denial, biblical lament brings raw pain before God, trusting that He listens and cares. The psalms of lament (e.g., Psalm 13, Psalm 88) model how to cry out honestly while anchoring hope in God's character. Such prayers reveal that perseverance is not about suppressing emotions; it is about directing them toward the One who can provide ultimate deliverance and comfort. As believers pour out grief, anger, or confusion, they simultaneously reaffirm their trust in God's overarching plan.

Encouragement from the cloud of witnesses

Hebrews 12:1–2 evokes a stirring image: a "great cloud of witnesses" surrounding believers, encouraging them to run the race with endurance. These witnesses refer to the faith heroes of the past, like Abel, Enoch, Abraham, Moses, and others who trusted God despite not receiving the full promise in their lifetime (Hebrews 11). Their stories inspire us to keep running, eyes fixed on

Jesus. In practical terms, recalling the testimonies of saints—both ancient and modern—provides a reservoir of inspiration. Their perseverance, often under far harsher conditions, shows that God's grace truly sustains the faithful to the end.

Transformative outcomes

Suffering, in the context of perseverance, can produce profound transformation. Trials expose hidden idols, test the depth of our convictions, and refine illusions of self-sufficiency. As believers emerge from hardships, they often carry deeper empathy, wisdom, and a sharpened sense of life's fragility. They also develop a clearer longing for heaven, recognizing that only in God's presence will every tear be wiped away (Revelation 21:4). Far from being wasted, these hardships become stepping stones toward greater Christlikeness and a more acute awareness of eternal realities.

6.3.2 Consistent Devotion

Faithfulness in ordinary moments

Pressing on in faith is not limited to dramatic trials or heroic feats; it also unfolds in the steady devotion of ordinary life. The daily routines of prayer, Scripture reading, fellowship, and ethical conduct may seem unimpressive. Yet Jesus frequently used agricultural metaphors—like seeds growing secretly (Mark 4:26–29)—to illustrate how God's kingdom advances imperceptibly until it bears fruit. The consistent believer who prays quietly each morning, shows kindness to strangers, and forgives petty offenses at work participates in a divine process. Over time, these habits accumulate spiritual momentum, shaping both personal character and communal impact.

Avoiding spiritual burnout

Consistency requires avoiding the extremes of complacency on one hand and spiritual burnout on the other. Some believers, enthused by a season of revival, push themselves into countless activities, only to lose focus when fatigue sets in. A healthy devotion finds rhythm and balance. Jesus Himself would minister to crowds, then withdraw to solitary places to pray (Luke 5:16). By pacing ourselves and respecting the limitations of body and mind, we sustain long-term service. This approach also includes trusting God's timing and refraining from the anxiety that tries to force outcomes.

The role of discipline

Discipline often carries negative connotations, but in a Christian context, it is a gateway to freedom. Structured routines of Bible meditation, corporate worship, and even fasting can guard against distractions and fleshly impulses. Over time, discipline fosters delight, as the believer experiences the joy of communion with God that far surpasses superficial pleasures. As Paul mentions in 1 Corinthians 9:25–27, athletes exercise discipline to obtain a perishable wreath, yet Christians discipline themselves for an imperishable crown. This is an eternal perspective at work, investing in practices that yield lifelong—indeed, eternal—benefits.

Handling spiritual plateaus

Even the most consistent believers face seasons of dryness or plateau, where spiritual growth seems to stall. In these times, reflection and humility are key. Perhaps new spiritual disciplines or a deeper engagement with community are needed. Or maybe God is teaching reliance on Him rather than on emotional experiences. The resolution is not to abandon devotion but to lean more intentionally into God's Word and the fellowship of believers, trusting the Holy Spirit to rekindle passion in due course. By persevering through these lulls, believers emerge with a faith unshaken by fluctuating feelings.

Strengthening others through example

Consistent devotion leaves a powerful legacy, not only personally but within the broader community of faith. Younger believers or seekers often watch how mature Christians handle monotony, criticism, or unfulfilled desires. When they observe someone who, despite disappointments, remains faithful in prayer and service, they gain tangible proof that God is worth trusting. In this way, consistency in devotion becomes a silent sermon that can speak more persuasively than eloquent preaching. It assures onlookers that the Christian walk is not mere hype but a solid, daily relationship with the Living God.

6.4. Encouraging Others Toward the Prize

6.4.1 Sharing Testimonies of Hope

The communal nature of hope

Hope, by its very nature, overflows. When a believer experiences a breakthrough—be it healing, deliverance from addiction, or a renewed sense of purpose—that testimony can ignite faith in others. Acts 14:27 records how Paul and Barnabas, upon returning from their missionary journey, gathered the church to "declare all that God had done with them." By recounting the miracles and open doors they had witnessed, they fortified the congregation's conviction that God was still actively at work. In similar fashion, modern believers share personal stories of God's faithfulness to stir the hearts of friends, family, and fellow church members.

The power of lived experience

Testimonies carry a persuasive weight that abstract arguments often lack. A man who survived years of substance abuse but found freedom in Christ can offer hope to others trapped in addiction. A widow who encountered God's comfort can encourage the grieving that healing is possible. These firsthand accounts do not merely convey doctrine; they exemplify transformation. As people see tangible evidence of redemption and restoration, they are inspired to believe that God can likewise meet their own needs. In effect, testimonies bridge the gap between biblical promises and lived reality.

Diverse formats of testimony

Sharing testimonies need not be confined to formal settings. While it is common to have testimony segments in church services, the exchange of testimonies can also happen organically—in small groups, over a meal, or through social media. Written testimonies, such as blog posts or personal devotionals, reach broader audiences. Documentary-style videos or podcasts can effectively capture someone's journey from despair to deliverance. Regardless of the medium, the key is authenticity: the willingness to reveal struggles and the raw process leading to victory, rather than presenting a polished or idealized version of events.

Guarding against sensationalism

As testimonies gain attention, a subtle temptation is to sensationalize and enhance spiritual experiences for dramatic effect. Yet Scripture cautions against elevating extraordinary signs over faithful living. When sharing testimonies, it is crucial to keep Christ at the center—His grace, His redemptive power, His glory.

This emphasis prevents the narrative from becoming a platform for self-promotion. John the Baptist's motto, "He must increase, but I must decrease" (John 3:30), remains a powerful corrective. Authentic testimonies aim to direct admiration toward God, strengthening communal faith in His power and goodness.

6.4.2 Building One Another Up

Fellowship as spiritual edification

The pursuit of the "ultimate prize" is not a solitary endeavor but one the church undertakes together. In Ephesians 4:15–16, Paul describes the body of Christ as joined and held together, with each part working properly to promote growth in love. This interdependence means that no believer is an island; we are called to uplift each other, both in word and deed. Whether through teaching, encouragement, or tangible support, we build one another up, ensuring that no one grows weary without someone to help them stand.

Practical encouragement

Words of affirmation might seem minor, but they carry significant weight in sustaining hope. A timely text message acknowledging someone's growth, a handwritten note praising their faithfulness, or a phone call that simply says, "I'm praying for you," can fuel perseverance. In a culture often marred by criticism or indifference, such simple gestures resonate deeply. Physical acts of service—like delivering meals during illness or assisting with childcare—likewise demonstrate the heart of Christ. By consistently meeting each other's needs, believers mirror the reciprocal care envisioned in the New Testament.

Correcting in love

113

Encouragement also involves gentle correction when necessary. Galatians 6:1–2 instructs that if someone is caught in sin, those who are spiritual should restore them in a spirit of gentleness. This accountability is not about judgment or moral superiority but about safeguarding one another from straying off the path to which God has called us. When approached humbly, loving confrontation can prevent small compromises from evolving into destructive habits. Such correction, rooted in grace and truth, helps each member remain focused on the eternal prize, unencumbered by hidden sins or drifting priorities.

Collaborative prayer and worship

Building one another up is powerfully expressed in corporate prayer and worship. When believers unite to worship, they acknowledge God's presence and recall His promises together. In seasons of trial, they strengthen each other's faith, forging a collective resilience. Likewise, intercessory prayer for one another fosters deep relational bonds. James 5:16 encourages believers to pray for one another "that you may be healed." While physical healing is part of this, the verse also hints at broader spiritual wholeness, affirming the importance of communal prayer in sustaining each believer's walk toward eternity.

Unity and witness

Finally, the unity that emerges from mutual edification serves as a powerful witness to the watching world. Jesus prayed that believers would be one, "so that the world may believe" (John 17:21). A church that stands in unity, supporting and encouraging its members, demonstrates the transformative power of the gospel. This unity is not uniformity—differences in personality, background, or spiritual maturity persist—but a shared commitment to spurring each other toward Christ's likeness. By loving each other deeply, believers collectively shine as lights pointing to the eternal hope found only in the Savior.

Conclusion

Throughout this chapter, we have observed that an eternal perspective is not an optional add-on to the Christian life but a *foundational orientation* that shapes how believers navigate every aspect of existence. By lifting our eyes beyond temporal circumstances, we discover a firm anchor for the soul: God's promise of everlasting fellowship with Him. This hope undergirds how we interpret suffering, how we prioritize daily tasks, and how we cultivate goals that reflect Christ's character rather than the world's fleeting ambitions.

The apostle Paul, reflecting on his own life, wrote, "I have fought the good fight, I have finished the race, I have kept the faith. Henceforth there is laid up for me the crown of righteousness" (2 Timothy 4:7–8). His words encapsulate a triumphant final chapter for the believer who keeps eternity in view. Like an athlete who endures rigorous training, the Christian invests heart and soul into the race of faith, confident of the incomparable prize awaiting at the finish line. This is not reserved for the spiritual elite, but for all who love the Lord's appearing.

As this chapter concludes, reflect on the ways you might deepen your own eternal perspective. Are there distractions or anxieties that keep your gaze locked on the here and now? Might there be an opportunity to redirect your ambitions toward serving others in view of God's kingdom? Are there fellow believers who need your encouragement or gentle correction to keep running their race well? In answering these questions, remember that God's Spirit is ever present to guide, empower, and comfort you in the quest for that ultimate prize: the fullness of life in His unending presence.

May this vision embolden you to live fully in the present while pressing onward with unwavering hope, anticipating the glorious day when faith becomes sight.

Chapter 7: Selfish vs. Selfless Love: Living with a Christlike Heart

Love stands at the core of the Christian faith. From Genesis to Revelation, we find God's love woven into every redemptive act. Jesus Himself taught that the greatest commandments center on loving God wholeheartedly and loving others as ourselves. Yet in a fallen world, believers constantly grapple with the tension between selfish and selfless expressions of love. On one hand, our culture fosters self-centeredness, enticing us to prioritize personal gain, convenience, and gratification. On the other hand, Christ calls us to a self-giving devotion that echoes His own sacrificial care for humanity.

In this chapter, we will examine the stark contrast between these two types of love, unveiling how *selfish love* devalues others and perpetuates relational discord, while *selfless love*—rooted in Christ's example—sparks spiritual growth, nurtures unity, and transforms our daily interactions. We begin by recognizing self-serving tendencies and clarifying the essence of sacrificial concern for others. We then explore Christlike love in action, unpacking its tangible expressions of compassion and empathy. In the following sections, we address the common barriers—such as pride, insecurity, and unresolved conflict—that obstruct genuine love, and learn how reconciliation and forgiveness pave the way to deeper spiritual vitality. Finally, we turn to practical ways of living out selflessness in real-world contexts, highlighting how service to others, humility, and a sustained focus on God's glory create a lifestyle that reflects the heart of Christ.

7.1. Contrasting Two Types of Love

7.1.1 Recognizing Self-Serving Tendencies

The subtlety of selfish motives

 Many believers sincerely desire to love others, yet find themselves repeatedly drawn to motives that revolve around self. This dynamic can be deceptive, as *selfishness* often masquerades behind outward kindness or social politeness. For instance, a person might volunteer at church primarily to receive praise, or become friendly to a neighbor in hopes of gaining favors. While these actions appear commendable, the underlying driver remains personal benefit. In 1 Corinthians 4:5, Paul reminds believers that God "will disclose the purposes of the heart," indicating that true motives—however hidden—matter to our Lord.

Cultural reinforcements of self-focus

 Modern society unwittingly amplifies these self-serving leanings. Advertisements promise immediate fulfillment, social media can foster narcissism, and certain pop psychology movements promote self-actualization as the highest good. Though not all of these impulses are inherently evil, when left unchecked, they encourage a worldview in which personal comfort and ambition trump the welfare of others. Romans 12:2 cautions against conforming to the world's values, highlighting that we must constantly realign our mindset with God's perspective rather than the prevailing cultural ethos.

Consequences in relationships

Relationally, selfish love tends toward transactional exchanges. It calculates whether another person "deserves" kindness, offers help only if reciprocation seems likely, or quietly weighs personal advantages. Over time, such conditional love sows distrust. Close friendships remain shallow, marriages fracture under the pressure of unmet expectations, and church communities splinter as members prioritize their own agendas. This erosion stems from love that, at its core, is fueled by the question, *"What do I get out of this?"* When personal gain is central, genuine intimacy and sacrificial service become rare.

Blurring boundaries of self-care

Self-care does play a valid role in maintaining emotional and physical health; indeed, Jesus Himself took time to rest, withdrawing from the crowds to pray (Luke 5:16). However, selfishness manipulates this principle into a lifestyle fixated on self-protection and avoidance of sacrificial demands. The difference lies in *intent*: biblical self-care aims to replenish us for further service, whereas a self-serving mindset elevates personal comfort as an end in itself. Recognizing where legitimate self-stewardship crosses into indulgent self-absorption is essential for cultivating a healthy, outward-directed life.

A call to repentance

Ultimately, identifying self-serving tendencies requires humility. Like David, who prayed, "Search me, O God, and know my heart" (Psalm 139:23–24), believers must invite the Holy Spirit to expose hidden vanity or manipulation. This awareness is not meant to induce despair but to lead us toward repentance, cleansing, and transformation. When we take an honest inventory of motives, we begin a journey away from hollow, self-oriented love and toward a selfless, Christlike approach that puts others' well-being first.

7.1.2 Understanding Sacrificial Concern for Others

The biblical definition of selfless love

Scripture's vision of love stands in stark contrast to the world's definitions. Jesus summarizes this love succinctly in John 15:13: "Greater love has no one than this, that someone lay down his life for his friends." While this verse directly foreshadows the crucifixion, it also captures a broader principle: *selfless love sacrifices personal comfort, privilege, and sometimes rights for the sake of another's good.* This principle permeates the New Testament, revealing that genuine love seeks the other's welfare even at personal cost.

Christ as the ultimate model

Christ's life on earth provides the ultimate model of selfless love. From healing the sick to feeding the hungry, from teaching the crowds to washing His disciples' feet (John 13:12–15), Jesus consistently placed others' needs above His own. The greatest display, of course, occurred at Calvary, where He willingly suffered to redeem humanity. Believers are thus called to "walk in love, as Christ loved us and gave himself up for us" (Ephesians 5:2). This call compels us beyond superficial compassion, challenging us to take on burdens, endure inconvenience, and invest in people who may never repay us.

Love's inseparable link to holiness

Selfless love aligns with holiness, for it is rooted in God's own character. The apostle John declares that "God is love" (1 John 4:8), while the Old Testament constantly underscores His holiness (Leviticus 19:2). Far from being contradictory, these traits intertwine: God's love is pure, just, and righteous, seeking the best for creatures without violating His moral perfection. Emulating such love requires believers to grow in moral discernment—knowing how to balance compassion with truth, mercy with accountability. This synergy ensures that we do not mistake permissiveness for love, nor hardness for holiness.

Evidence of spiritual maturity

Sacrificial concern for others also signals spiritual maturity. While new believers may earnestly desire to love but find themselves continually stumbling into pride or impatience, those who have walked with Christ over time grow increasingly adept at living out self-giving love. First Corinthians 3:1–3 contrasts those who remain in spiritual infancy—marked by jealousy and strife—with believers who mature into a life shaped by love and unity. Progress in selfless love thus reflects the transforming power of the Holy Spirit, who aligns our hearts with God's priorities.

7.2. Christlike Love in Action

7.2.1 Tangible Expressions of Compassion

Jesus' example of practical mercy

Perhaps the most striking hallmark of Christ's ministry was His consistent engagement with people's immediate needs. When lepers approached Him for healing, He did not hesitate (Luke 17:11–14). When the crowd grew hungry, He fed them (Mark 8:1–9). In each instance, Jesus brought tangible relief, modeling a compassion that went beyond words. Today, believers mirror this selfless love through acts of care: delivering groceries to a struggling neighbor, tutoring a child from a low-income family, or providing respite to exhausted caregivers. The focus is on meeting real needs, demonstrating God's concern for the totality of a person's well-being—spiritual, emotional, and physical.

The difference between pity and empathy

An important aspect of such compassion is the shift from *pity* to *empathy*. Pity merely observes suffering from a distance, occasionally stirring a brief wave of sadness or guilt. Empathy, in contrast, steps into the other's experience, seeking to understand their feelings and perspectives. Romans 12:15 instructs believers to "weep with those who weep," emphasizing solidarity in both joy and sorrow. Empathy motivates deeper, more heartfelt action. Instead of tossing spare change at a problem, it prompts you to learn someone's story, forging a relationship that can lead to lasting transformation.

Practical humility in service

Acts of compassion necessarily involve humility. In John 13:14, after washing His disciples' feet, Jesus told them, "You also ought to wash one another's feet." Foot washing, an act typically assigned to the lowest servant, symbolized radical humility. Serving in ways that society deems "menial" can be uncomfortable. Yet such tasks reflect a heart freed from pride. This might mean cleaning restrooms after church, helping with yard work for an elderly neighbor, or offering rides to a coworker without a car. The point is not the task's prestige but the sincerity of love fueling it.

Long-term commitment to compassion

While spontaneous gestures of kindness are valuable, selfless love also requires *consistency*. Many needs persist over weeks, months, or years—especially in cases of chronic illness, disability, or systemic poverty. Initially, believers might respond with enthusiasm, only to fade away once the novelty wears off. True compassion perseveres. Galatians 6:9 advises us "not to grow weary of doing good," acknowledging that weariness is a real temptation. Maintaining a long-term commitment—sponsoring a child's education through a reputable ministry, regularly visiting a lonely neighbor, or tutoring at an underfunded school year after year—testifies to the enduring nature of Christlike love.

Avoiding 'savior complex'

When stepping into compassionate service, believers must guard against a "savior complex." This arises when helping others becomes entangled with self-aggrandizement, imagining oneself as the hero of every story. Authentic love seeks to empower recipients, honor their dignity, and point them to the true Savior— Jesus Christ. Volunteers or donors who overshadow the recipient's agency, or boast of their own generosity, dilute the essence of sacrificial love. By contrast, believers who quietly persist in humble service bring glory to God, not themselves, while genuinely uplifting those in need.

7.2.2 Cultivating Empathy and Kindness

Empathy as a learned virtue

Empathy does not always come naturally; it can be cultivated through deliberate effort. Philippians 2:3–4 exhorts believers to "count others more significant than yourselves," actively considering other people's needs. This mindset shift grows with practice. A first step is simply to listen more closely when someone shares a burden, resisting the urge to interject personal anecdotes or advice. Another is to research issues affecting marginalized groups—learning about the challenges they face—so we can respond with informed compassion rather than assumptions or ignorance.

Kind words and their power

Proverbs 16:24 teaches that "Gracious words are like a honeycomb, sweetness to the soul." Kindness often starts with speech—an affirming note, an encouraging text, or a simple compliment. In an era of online spats and face-to-face confrontations, believers who guard their tongues against gossip, criticism, or sarcastic jabs stand out. Words can tear down or build up. By consistently offering kind words, we demonstrate respect for each person's worth as God's creation. Moreover, kind speech fosters an environment of trust, paving the way for deeper relationships rooted in mutual honor.

Creating a culture of hospitality

A practical extension of empathy and kindness is hospitality. Opening your home for a shared meal, offering a safe space to someone in crisis, or hosting a small group Bible study fosters community. Rather than focusing on perfect decor or elaborate dishes, biblical hospitality prioritizes warmth and authenticity (1 Peter 4:9). When newcomers or vulnerable individuals sense genuine acceptance, they see a reflection of God's welcoming heart. Hospitality can be especially transformative in multicultural settings, bridging cultural gaps through the simple act of sharing food and stories.

Conflict resolution through empathy

Empathy also transforms how we address conflict. Instead of demonizing the other person, selfless love urges us to consider their perspective. James 1:19 advises believers to be "quick to hear, slow to speak, slow to anger." This principle counters the reflex to defend our pride or dismiss the other's viewpoint. Approaching disagreements with empathy can defuse tension and foster mutual understanding, even if total agreement remains elusive. Such grace in conflict resolution testifies to a love that values reconciliation over "winning."

Small acts with great impact

Finally, empathy and kindness do not require dramatic gestures. A phone call to check on someone's well-being, a handwritten note after a busy season, or an offer to run errands for a neighbor can have a significant emotional impact. These small acts, performed with consistency, weave a fabric of care that sustains relationships over time. As Jesus pointed out in Luke 16:10, faithfulness in the little things reflects readiness for greater responsibilities. Cultivating empathy in seemingly minor moments trains our hearts to respond with Christlike compassion whenever needs arise.

7.3. Overcoming Barriers to Genuine Love

7.3.1 Pride and Insecurity

Twin obstacles to selfless love

Pride and insecurity might seem like opposites, yet both inhibit genuine love. Pride inflates our sense of self-importance, making others' needs appear trivial. Insecurity, by contrast, can breed an excessive focus on personal shortcomings or perceived rejection, also hindering the capacity to serve wholeheartedly. Both states revolve around *self* rather than God, distorting our ability to give or receive love.

Biblical warnings against pride

Scripture abounds with warnings about pride, from Proverbs 16:18 ("Pride goes before destruction") to Jesus' chastisement of the Pharisees' self-righteousness (Luke 18:9–14). Pride blinds us to the grace we continually need, fostering a sense of entitlement. People under pride's grip often feel threatened by others' achievements or manipulate relationships to preserve a façade of superiority. This attitude stifles empathy and fuels tension. True spiritual progress requires acknowledging that "God opposes the proud but gives grace to the humble" (James 4:6).

Insecurity's paralyzing effect

On the other hand, insecurity leads us to question our worth, overshadowing the fact that God values us immensely (Isaiah 43:4). It can manifest in constant comparison, jealousy, or withdrawal from relationships to avoid potential rejection. Because selfless love requires courage to reach beyond ourselves, insecurity can paralyze us in fear. We may doubt our ability to help, or suspect that others will not appreciate our efforts. Over time, this fear-driven mindset can make us hesitant to form meaningful connections.

Cultivating a secure identity in Christ

The antidote to both pride and insecurity lies in anchoring our identity firmly in Christ. Pride is dismantled when we recognize that all gifts, talents, and resources come from God and are meant for His glory (1 Corinthians 4:7). Insecurity is overcome by grasping that our acceptance rests not on performance but on God's unmerited love (Ephesians 1:4–5). As we internalize these truths, we stand on secure ground, free to invest in others without fear of losing ourselves or needing constant validation.

7.3.2 Reconciliation and Forgiveness

Broken relationships as barriers

Resentment, unresolved anger, and bitterness form some of the most powerful barriers to Christlike love. Even believers committed to selflessness can stumble when wounded by betrayal, injustice, or heartbreak. The resulting grudges or emotional walls corrode our ability to offer compassion. In Matthew 5:23–24, Jesus insists that worship must be preceded by reconciliation, underscoring how relational rifts impede true fellowship with God.

The biblical call to forgiveness

Scripture consistently elevates forgiveness as a core expression of God's redemptive love. Colossians 3:13 instructs, "forgive each other; as the Lord has forgiven you, so you also must forgive." This command rests on the reality of God's grace toward us; because Christ canceled our immense debt of sin, we are compelled to release the debts we hold against others. Far from minimizing wrongdoing, biblical forgiveness trusts that God is the ultimate judge. It frees believers from the poison of bitterness, making space for grace to restore or at least relieve relational tension.

Misconceptions about forgiveness

Many misunderstand forgiveness as condoning harmful behavior or pretending the hurt never happened. True forgiveness, however, acknowledges the severity of the offense while choosing not to seek vengeance. It does not automatically entail reestablishing trust or close friendship; boundaries may still be necessary, especially in cases of abuse. But it dissolves the desire for retribution and opens a path for healing—both for the forgiver and potentially for the offender, if repentance occurs. In short, forgiveness lays the groundwork for possible reconciliation while preserving the forgiver's spiritual integrity.

The role of confrontation and repentance

While believers must cultivate a willingness to forgive, Scripture also recognizes the importance of confronting sin. Luke 17:3 states, "If your brother sins, rebuke him, and if he repents, forgive him." This verse underscores that love does not sweep wrongdoing under the rug. True reconciliation often requires honest dialogue about the hurt caused. When the offender repents, forgiveness can be fully embraced, clearing a path to restored fellowship. However, even if the offender remains unrepentant, we can still release bitterness before God, entrusting final justice to His hands and guarding our hearts from corrosive resentment.

Healing through Christ's example

Ultimately, reconciliation and forgiveness draw from Christ's atoning work on the cross. Ephesians 2:14–16 depicts Jesus as our peace, breaking down the dividing wall of hostility. Whether the rift is between individuals or entire communities, God's grace has the power to mend. By reflecting on Christ's sacrifice—the innocent slain for the guilty—believers are reminded that no chasm is too vast for divine love to bridge. As we lay down grievances at the foot of the cross, we discover a fresh capacity to extend mercy, even when it defies human logic.

7.4. Living Out Selflessness

7.4.1 Practical Service Opportunities

Finding your mission field

Selfless love becomes more than a concept when integrated into our daily lives. Each believer inhabits distinct spheres of influence— a workplace, neighborhood, family, hobby group—where God may be calling them to serve. Rather than waiting for the perfect mission trip or a grand ministry title, we can ask, *What are the needs right where I am? Who are the people God has placed before me?* Often, the mission field is the cubicle next door, the playground where local kids gather, or the homeless shelter across town. By looking with spiritual eyes, we discover that chances to practice selflessness abound.

Creative ways to serve

Service extends beyond standard volunteer roles. Some might turn a creative passion into an outreach—painting murals at a shelter, teaching music to underprivileged youth, or sewing clothes for families in crisis. Others find meaning in administrative tasks that free pastors and church staff to focus on discipleship. Younger believers might commit to tutoring classmates struggling with certain subjects. Whether broad or specialized, each act of service, done in love, reflects the body of Christ working as a cohesive whole. First Peter 4:10 emphasizes this diversity: "As each has received a gift, use it to serve one another, as good stewards of God's varied grace."

Challenges and sacrifice

Genuine service often requires stepping beyond comfort zones. Volunteering at a prison ministry may provoke fear or discomfort. Helping in a crisis pregnancy center could invite criticism from certain social circles. Even simpler tasks—like regularly mowing a neighbor's lawn—demand time and energy one might prefer to spend on personal hobbies. Yet Jesus' words in Mark 10:45 ring clear: "For even the Son of Man came not to be served but to serve." This does not mean neglecting proper boundaries or rest, but it does call believers to hold convenience loosely, embracing the rigors of authentic love.

Working together in the community

While individual initiatives matter, collaborative efforts can multiply impact. Church groups might sponsor a local school, mobilizing resources to fund supplies, mentorship programs, or building repairs. A small group can adopt a local nursing home, providing regular visits and companionship. Collaboration also fosters accountability and prevents burnout, as the burden of service is shared rather than carried by a lone individual. Moreover, working alongside other believers cultivates fellowship grounded in a shared mission, strengthening relationships and encouraging one another in faith.

Measuring results by eternal standards

Finally, measuring the fruit of service according to worldly metrics—money raised, numbers reached—can be misleading. While quantitative data can be helpful, the deeper question is whether lives are being touched by Christ's love. A single conversation that leads someone closer to salvation, or a consistent presence that helps a struggling teenager gain confidence, may have more eternal weight than large-scale events. As Galatians 5:6 reminds us, "the only thing that counts is faith expressing itself through love." When love, rooted in genuine concern, permeates our service, each act, whether seemingly small or large, resonates with eternal significance.

7.4.2 Sustaining an Others-Centered Lifestyle

Establishing spiritual rhythms

Maintaining selfless love over the long haul requires more than raw effort. Believers must cultivate spiritual rhythms—prayer, reflection on Scripture, corporate worship—that keep the focus on God's heart and power. Without these, altruistic energy can fade into fatigue or resentment. Daily prayer reorients the heart toward God's kingdom, asking Him to direct our interactions. Studying biblical narratives of servanthood, such as Ruth's loyalty or Paul's missionary sacrifices, can rekindle inspiration. Corporate worship fosters accountability as we gather with fellow believers, sharing testimonies of how God is moving through acts of love.

Balancing self-care and service

Though love is sacrificial, it is not reckless self-neglect. Jesus Himself honored rest, as indicated by His frequent retreats for prayer. In Mark 6:31, He invites His disciples, "Come away by yourselves to a desolate place and rest a while." Achieving a healthy balance ensures that prolonged service does not drain us to the point of spiritual or emotional collapse. Periods of genuine Sabbath—free from ministry obligations—replenish energy and perspective. Likewise, seeking pastoral support or Christian counseling can help process the emotional burdens that often accompany consistent service to those in dire need.

Avoiding compassion fatigue

Compassion fatigue looms as a real threat for believers heavily involved in caregiving or crisis ministry. Overexposure to pain—be it in a hospital ward, homeless outreach, or missions field—can dull emotional sensitivity, leaving one feeling numb or apathetic. The solution is not cynicism but intentional self-reflection and seeking refreshing fellowship. Journaling about what God is teaching through each encounter or debriefing with a small group can release pent-up emotions. Additionally, acknowledging that *we* are not the ultimate savior fosters healthy detachment; our role is to sow seeds of love, trusting God for the harvest.

Continual growth in humility

Sustaining an others-centered lifestyle hinges on **humility**. Even after years of faithful service, believers remain susceptible to pride, complacency, or moral compromise. Regularly examining motives—asking if love remains the driving force—keeps us tethered to the cross. Philippians 2:3–8, which praises Christ's humility in becoming human and dying on a cross, provides a powerful template. As we meditate on this passage, we remind ourselves that all glory belongs to God. Our call is to reflect Jesus, not compete for accolades or slip into self-pity when recognition does not come.

Conclusion

At its essence, the Christian life centers on love—love for God, love for fellow believers, and even love for those who stand opposed to us. Yet as we have seen, love is not a simple, universal concept. The difference between selfish and selfless love is profound, shaping whether our relationships revolve around personal gain or genuine concern for another's good. In a society enthralled by individualism, pursuing selfless love stands as a countercultural act of obedience to Christ's example.

Ultimately, living with a Christlike heart calls us to cultivate a disposition of humility, sensitivity, and unwavering commitment to others' well-being. It rejects the world's transactional approach, choosing instead to bestow grace freely. In doing so, we not only mirror Jesus' character but actively contribute to the kingdom's expansion. Our hospitality, empathy, and courage in loving even difficult people become living testimonies to the transformative grace of God.

Such a lifestyle is not a one-time event but a continual invitation to align with heaven's priorities. Each morning, believers can ask: *How might I extend God's love today? Whose burdens can I share, whose hopes can I nurture, whose sorrows can I alleviate?* As we take these small steps of obedience, we embody a love that is patient, kind, and free from envy or selfish ambition (1 Corinthians 13:4–5). Over time, our communities see fewer lonely neighbors, fewer broken families, and fewer neglected outcasts—evidence that the body of Christ is truly reflecting its Head.

May the Holy Spirit guide each of us into deeper expressions of compassion and service, enabling a fresh demonstration of selfless love in every sphere of influence. As we deny ourselves, pick up our cross daily, and follow Jesus (Luke 9:23), we discover that our hearts, once prone to selfish desires, are increasingly conformed to

His. And in this transformation lies the profound joy of participating in God's redemptive work—one act of selfless love at a time.

Chapter 8: Called vs. Chosen Life: Walking in Your Divine Purpose

From Genesis to Revelation, Scripture brims with accounts of people selected for specific tasks in God's unfolding story—Abraham, Moses, Deborah, David, Esther, Paul, and countless others. Each was called to a unique mission, yet not all stepped into that call in the same way or with the same outcome. The notion of being "called" by God holds a central place in Christian discipleship, but there is also a thread woven through the Bible about being chosen, indicating a further dimension of divine selection and purpose. Understanding these two concepts—and how they intersect—can radically shape how we view our life's work, relationships, and ultimate destiny in Christ.

This chapter explores the difference between being called and chosen, showing why these terms matter for everyday believers. We begin by defining the idea of a **calling** and why God extends various invitations to His people, followed by a look at what it means to be chosen—selected by God for a unique role or destiny.

8.1. Defining Calling and Choice

8.1.1 Understanding God's Invitation

Scriptural foundations of calling

In Scripture, the term "calling" can signify God's broader invitation to salvation or a more specific vocational summons. For instance, Paul writes, "God...called you into His own kingdom and glory" (1 Thessalonians 2:12). This highlights the universal call extended to all who would follow Christ. On the other hand, certain individuals receive more specialized calls: Abraham to leave his homeland (Genesis 12:1–3), Amos the shepherd to become a prophet (Amos 7:14–15), and the Twelve disciples to proclaim the gospel (Luke 9:1–6). Such stories reveal a spectrum, from the general to the particular, all orchestrated by a sovereign God who integrates countless threads into His redemptive tapestry.

The nature of divine summons

God's call often arrives in ways we don't expect, breaking into ordinary routines. Gideon was threshing wheat when an angel hailed him as a "mighty man of valor" (Judges 6:11–12). Elisha was plowing a field when Elijah called him to prophetic ministry (1 Kings 19:19). This pattern suggests that your daily tasks—mundane as they may seem—can be the setting for a pivotal encounter with God's purpose. A calling is not necessarily about hearing an audible voice or seeing a burning bush; it may emerge gradually through prayer, Scripture, counsel from mature believers, and a growing conviction of your role in God's kingdom.

Responding with reverence

When we speak of a "call," we're not talking about a casual invitation. The biblical concept conveys a profound sense of divine authority. This seriousness is echoed when Jonah resists God's command to preach in Nineveh (Jonah 1:1–3), leading to dire consequences until he realigns with God's will. Even Jeremiah, who felt too young to speak for God, eventually realized that divine calling supersedes human limitations (Jeremiah 1:5–7). Reverence for God's authority means approaching our calling with humility, acknowledging that it comes from the Creator who sees the end from the beginning.

Common misconceptions

Some believers assume that only pastors, missionaries, or worship leaders have a genuine "calling." Yet Scripture affirms that every Christian is summoned to a meaningful role—"You are a chosen race, a royal priesthood" (1 Peter 2:9)—encompassing all facets of life, from the workplace to the family setting. Another misconception is that calling always aligns with personal preferences or talents. While God certainly uses our gifts (Romans 12:6–8), He may also call us into areas that stretch us, requiring us to rely on His power rather than our comfort zone. Rejecting these misconceptions broadens our perspective, allowing us to see that God's invitation extends to every believer, in every context.

8.1.2 Embracing the Reality of Being Chosen

The biblical concept of "chosen"

Throughout Scripture, specific individuals and communities are described as "chosen" by God. Deuteronomy 7:6, for instance, depicts Israel as "a people holy to the LORD," chosen to be His treasured possession. In the New Testament, Jesus tells His disciples, "You did not choose Me, but I chose you and appointed you" (John 15:16). This language points to God's sovereign decision to set someone apart for a particular role. While calling suggests an invitation, being chosen emphasizes God's initiative—His decision to equip and appoint whomever He wills for specific tasks or blessings.

Selected for a purpose

Why does God choose certain people for unique assignments? Often, it's not about personal merit or extraordinary skill; rather, He chooses the humble, the unexpected, or those society might overlook. Consider David, an unassuming shepherd whom God selected as king (1 Samuel 16:1–13). Or Mary, a young Jewish girl in a modest town, chosen to bear the Messiah (Luke 1:26–38). Their stories affirm that divine choice is intimately linked to God's gracious plan. He looks beyond outward appearances and discerns hearts willing to obey, thus fulfilling His overarching purposes in the world.

The tension between called and chosen

The Gospels contain the famous statement, "Many are called, but few are chosen" (Matthew 22:14). This verse has sparked considerable theological reflection; and it suggests that while God's general call to repentance and faith in Christ goes out to many, those who respond genuinely and align themselves with His will become part of the "chosen." Another perspective holds that "chosen" references deeper levels of spiritual fruitfulness or specialized service in the kingdom. In either case, the tension highlights a distinction between hearing an invitation from God and truly stepping into it with surrender and perseverance.

The privilege and responsibility of the chosen

Being chosen carries both privilege and responsibility. On one hand, there is deep assurance in knowing God specifically appointed you for a task—He is with you, supplying wisdom and grace. On the other hand, it means surrendering personal agendas, accepting that your life is not your own. Paul exemplifies this dynamic. Chosen to be an apostle to the Gentiles (Galatians 1:15–16), he faced shipwrecks, beatings, and imprisonment while fulfilling his mandate (2 Corinthians 11:23–27). Nevertheless, he counted it joy to pour himself out for Christ. In a similar way, every believer who senses God's unique hand upon them must weigh the cost and privilege of that calling.

Navigating doubts about being chosen

Many Christians wrestle with doubt: *Am I really chosen? Does God truly have a special plan for me?* Although not everyone is called to high-profile leadership, each believer can rest in the truth that God has set them apart (2 Timothy 1:9). The question is less about exalting ourselves as "chosen" and more about faithfully pursuing whatever God places before us. When anxious, remember that Scripture repeatedly affirms God's love for His people, from the least to the greatest. The best antidote to uncertainty is diligent faithfulness, trusting that as we walk in obedience, He reveals His sovereign appointments in ways we may not initially foresee.

8.2. Recognizing Your Unique Purpose

8.2.1 Personal Giftings and Passions

Identifying spiritual gifts

A foundational step toward walking in your calling and chosen role is understanding your **spiritual gifts**. Passages like 1 Corinthians 12:4–11 and 1 Peter 4:10–11 list various gifts—teaching, hospitality, encouragement, administration, prophecy, and more. These gifts are bestowed by the Holy Spirit for the edification of the Church. While some believers discover their gifts early in their faith journey, others only realize them gradually. Testing yourself in different ministry settings, seeking feedback from mature Christians, and prayerfully asking the Holy Spirit for guidance can help you discern the gifts entrusted to you.

Natural talents and learned skills

In addition to spiritual gifts, God often works through your natural talents and learned skills. A musician's aptitude can become an avenue for worship; a knack for networking can translate into community outreach, and a passion for technology can be harnessed for missionary training programs. Even past experiences of hardship can shape unique empathy or resilience that God uses for kingdom impact (2 Corinthians 1:3–4). Recognizing these abilities is not about self-glorification but stewarding them for God's glory. It requires humility to remember that "every good gift...is from above" (James 1:17).

The role of passion in discernment

While not every passion equates to a God-given calling, significant alignment often occurs between what we love and what God calls us to do. Nehemiah's passionate burden for Jerusalem's broken walls (Nehemiah 1:3–4) led him to spearhead a rebuilding project, blending fervor with practical leadership. Similarly, if you find yourself consistently drawn to address a particular social injustice, serve a certain demographic, or express creativity in a specific medium, it could signal part of your divine purpose. Prayerful reflection and wise counsel help distinguish fleeting interests from genuine passions that align with Scripture's overarching mission.

Synergy of gifts and passions

True synergy arises when spiritual gifts, natural talents, and passionate concerns converge in service to God's kingdom. For instance, a believer with a spiritual gift of teaching, an aptitude for technology, and a passion for evangelism might create online discipleship resources that reach far beyond local boundaries. Another, gifted in mercy and skilled in medical care, might serve in a healthcare mission where compassion and expertise merge seamlessly. This synergy brings deep fulfillment and fruitfulness, turning tasks into meaningful contributions that extend God's love.

Avoiding comparison

A common pitfall arises when believers compare their gifts or passions with others'. The body of Christ thrives on diversity (Romans 12:4–5), and each part has a specific function. Fixating on another person's calling can breed envy or discouragement. Instead, celebrate the variety of callings within the Church. Embrace your distinct role, trusting that God orchestrates these differences for the collective good. By focusing on faithfulness rather than comparison, you free your mind to celebrate others' successes while wholeheartedly pursuing your unique path.

8.2.2 Confirming Calling Through Scripture and Prayer

The Word as a guide

Though personal desire and giftedness are valuable indicators, the surest way to confirm a calling is through God's Word. Psalm

119:105 likens Scripture to a lamp guiding our path. Its pages contain timeless principles about moral character, service, and devotion to God, helping us evaluate potential opportunities against biblical truth. For example, if a particular endeavor conflicts with clear scriptural mandates—like integrity, purity, or humility—it can't be God's calling, no matter how appealing it appears. Conversely, a direction that fosters spiritual growth, reflects Christlike compassion, and aligns with God's kingdom values likely resonates with His leading.

Devoted prayer and listening

Prayer stands as another vital key in discerning divine assignments. In Luke 6:12–13, Jesus spent an entire night in prayer before choosing the Twelve. That pattern underscores the seriousness with which we should approach decisions of calling. Regular, consistent prayer fosters sensitivity to the Holy Spirit's nudge and fosters trust in God's sovereignty. Just as importantly, prayer is not merely monologue but dialogue. Making space for silence, journaling, or reflective retreats can create room for God's subtle confirmations to emerge.

Seeking counsel from godly mentors

God often speaks through the wisdom of mentors and spiritual leaders. Moses initially resisted his calling, but he eventually benefited from Jethro's counsel about leadership structure (Exodus 18:13–24). Paul, after his Damascus Road encounter, spent time with the disciples at Damascus and later in Jerusalem, receiving guidance and validation for his ministry (Acts 9:19–28). Similarly, believers today benefit from seeking mature believers' input on major decisions, gleaning from their experiences and biblical insight. Wise counsel can confirm or refine what we perceive as

God's direction, providing a safety net against rash or misguided moves.

Interpreting open and closed doors

Practical circumstances—open or closed doors—also play a role. At times, what seems like a perfect ministry role or career path slams shut unexpectedly. Other times, opportunities arise that we never actively pursued. The apostle Paul experienced this dynamic when the Holy Spirit prevented him from preaching in Asia and Bithynia, redirecting him to Macedonia (Acts 16:6–10). While not every closed door is a divine "no" forever, it can signal that God has a different timeline or route in mind. Holding our plans loosely and trusting God's timing is essential for aligning with His best.

Maintaining a flexible heart

Finally, confirming your calling requires a flexible heart, open to unexpected directions. Abraham had to leave the familiarity of Ur, not knowing the final destination (Hebrews 11:8–10). Likewise, you may find your calling evolves over time. A season of local church ministry may transition into overseas missions, or a corporate career may shift into nonprofit work. The crucial point is remaining pliable in God's hands, consistently re-evaluating, "Lord, is this still where You want me?" This humility paves the way for ongoing alignment with God's ever-unfolding purposes in and through you.

8.3. Obedience and Fulfillment

8.3.1 The Cost of Following God's Call

Biblical examples of costly obedience

No exploration of calling is complete without recognizing the sacrificial element that often accompanies it. Consider the prophet Hosea, commanded to marry a woman who would be unfaithful, becoming a living parable of God's love for unfaithful Israel (Hosea 1:2). Or think of Daniel, who faced a lion's den rather than abandon his devotion to God (Daniel 6:6–23). Their examples illustrate that obedience to divine call can bring trials, misunderstanding, or even persecution. In modern times, a missionary might leave a comfortable life to serve in a remote area, or a believer may lose social standing by upholding biblical ethics in a secular environment.

Embracing kingdom priorities over comfort

Obedience often requires dethroning personal comfort in favor of kingdom priorities. When Jesus says, "Whoever loses his life for My sake will find it" (Matthew 16:25), He implies that genuine discipleship upends conventional success metrics. A chosen or called life is not about chasing the easiest path; it's about unreserved alignment with God's will. This can involve relinquishing control of finances, relocating geographically, or surrendering personal ambitions. Yet paradoxically, it is in this surrender that believers experience profound fulfillment—knowing they are precisely where God wants them to be.

Facing opposition and doubt

Following God's call does not guarantee universal approval. Nehemiah's efforts to rebuild Jerusalem were opposed by local officials who mocked and threatened him (Nehemiah 4:1–3, 7–8). Similarly, Jesus' own family initially questioned His mission (Mark 3:21). Opposition can surface even within the Church, as well-meaning individuals might not grasp the radical nature of your calling. Such challenges test resolve, driving you to rely more deeply on God. While wise counsel remains vital, you must learn to discern constructive guidance from fear-driven dissuasion. Courage is often needed to press forward when circumstances or opinions try to undermine your conviction.

Counting the cost

Before wholeheartedly pursuing a calling, you must count the cost. In Luke 14:28–33, Jesus likens discipleship to a builder who calculates resources before starting a project. While we cannot anticipate every obstacle, we can prayerfully evaluate whether we're prepared to endure the rigors that obedience may entail. Counting the cost does not mean we fear failure; rather, it fosters sober commitment, ensuring that we do not embark on a path flippantly. Such honesty also guards us from disillusionment when hardships arise, reminding us that self-denial and perseverance form part of the Christian journey.

Divine provision in the midst of sacrifice

Despite these hardships, Scripture repeatedly assures believers of divine provision. Elijah, fleeing Jezebel's wrath, found sustenance by a ravine where ravens fed him (1 Kings 17:2–6). Paul, battered by trials, declared, "My God will supply every need of yours" (Philippians 4:19). These accounts affirm that while obedience may be costly, God meets us at every step. Provision may come in forms we least expect—a timely word of encouragement, financial help from an unlikely source, or supernatural peace during adversity. The knowledge that God walks with us fuels courage to press on in our calling.

8.3.2 Finding Joy in Sacrifice

Redefining fulfillment

A key misunderstanding is that sacrifice excludes joy. In reality, Scripture often pairs the two. The writer of Hebrews, reflecting on Jesus' journey to the cross, notes that "for the joy that was set before Him," He endured the cross (Hebrews 12:2). This example reveals that biblical joy is not superficial happiness dependent on ease but a deeper gladness rooted in obeying God and loving others. When we adopt this perspective, even the hardships associated with our calling can become channels of joy, knowing we participate in a greater story with eternal rewards.

The paradox of spiritual joy

Believers repeatedly encounter a paradox: the more we empty ourselves for God, the more He fills us with delight and purpose. Paul, writing from prison, speaks of rejoicing (Philippians 4:4), reflecting an internal buoyancy that no circumstance could quench. Similarly, you may find that the most strenuous aspects of your calling—long hours, challenging people, unforeseen setbacks— bring spiritual growth and a sense of holy satisfaction that cannot be replicated by worldly achievements. This joy is not naive about pain; it coexists with tears but refuses to be defeated by them.

Celebrating small victories

A practical way to cultivate joy is by celebrating small victories along the path of obedience. Whether it's a single person encouraged, a colleague showing curiosity about the gospel, or a community project making incremental progress—these milestones reflect God at work. In the Old Testament, altars were built to memorialize God's interventions (Genesis 12:7; Joshua 4:1– 9). Similarly, taking time to acknowledge God's faithfulness after each step fosters gratitude and rekindles motivation. Even if overall progress feels slow, these markers remind us that our labor is not in vain.

Communal dimensions of joy

Obedience and fulfillment are often enriched in community. Bearing one another's burdens (Galatians 6:2) means sharing joys as well. Celebrating testimonies within a small group or church setting can amplify delight and mutual encouragement. When your local fellowship recognizes God's hand in your calling—be it domestic missions, worship ministry, or neighborhood outreach— they can pray, support, and rejoice with you. This communal synergy also guards against isolation, which can lead to burnout or discouragement.

Longevity in ministry

Finally, finding joy in sacrifice is key to longevity in ministry. Many begin enthusiastically but fade as challenges mount. Those who nurture spiritual joy—through prayer, friendship, regular rest, and reflection on God's goodness—develop resilience that sustains them over the long haul. Instead of viewing daily tasks as drudgery, they see them as opportunities to experience God's presence and love. Such a lifestyle transforms obedience from a heavy yoke into a life-giving journey where trials and triumphs alike contribute to a rich tapestry of God's grace.

8.4. Impacting the World Around You

8.4.1 Serving the Church Community

Unity and diversity in the Body

Central to a called and chosen life is the commitment to edify the Church community. In 1 Corinthians 12:12–26, Paul likens the

Church to a human body, with each part fulfilling a distinct role. Eyes, hands, ears, and feet all have a function, and none can claim superiority. This metaphor underscores how every believer's calling intersects with corporate life. Whether you're chosen for teaching, administration, hospitality, prayer, or another area, your contribution fosters healthy unity and mutual edification. Ignoring or undervaluing your role creates dysfunction, like a body missing a vital limb.

Cultivating a servant attitude

Jesus taught that greatness in His kingdom arises not from lording authority but from serving humbly (Mark 10:42–45). This principle applies within the Church: those who are called or chosen to lead must do so with an attitude of servant-leadership, placing others' well-being before their own ambition. Similarly, those called to behind-the-scenes tasks—like cleaning facilities or maintaining church finances—demonstrate love by ensuring that the broader congregation operates smoothly. Such humility cements relationships and fosters an environment where diverse callings flourish harmoniously.

Mentoring and discipleship

One overlooked yet powerful way to impact the Church community is by investing in mentorship and discipleship. Paul mentored Timothy (2 Timothy 1:2), passing on theological truths, practical ministry advice, and personal encouragement. Even if you're not in a formal leadership position, you can mentor newer believers in prayer, Bible study, or faith application. This relational passing of the baton amplifies your calling far beyond what you could accomplish alone. If your gift lies in teaching, train others to teach. If you excel in administration, empower younger believers to handle organizational tasks. Such generational continuity ensures the Church remains strong and vibrant.

Responding to local needs

A called or chosen life also discerns pressing needs within the congregation. Is there a shortage of support for single parents, seniors, or new immigrants? Are worship services accessible for people with disabilities? By observing these gaps and aligning them with your gifts, you can launch initiatives—from childcare ministries to translation services—that embody God's compassion. Rather than waiting for a pastor's directive, believers can proactively propose solutions, trusting that God who orchestrates callings also provides creativity and resources.

Measuring fruitfulness

While numeric growth or visible success can be encouraging, the ultimate measure of Church impact is spiritual fruit—transformed hearts, deepening devotion to Christ, and an outflow of love that touches the surrounding community. In John 13:35, Jesus states, "By this all people will know that you are My disciples, if you have love for one another." A flourishing congregation, united in service, becomes a living testimony to God's power. Your specific calling contributes to this environment, enabling deeper discipleship and a compelling witness to a watching world.

8.4.2 Contributing to Societal Transformation

Biblical examples of cultural impact

Throughout Scripture, God's servants often influenced society in remarkable ways. Joseph's calling led him to interpret Pharaoh's dreams, implementing policies that saved nations from famine

(Genesis 41:38–49). Esther risked her life in a royal context to protect her people from genocide (Esther 4:14). Daniel's public faithfulness in Babylon shaped imperial decrees acknowledging God's sovereignty (Daniel 6:25–27). These accounts remind us that a divine calling can have ripple effects in the political, economic, or cultural spheres. Modern Christians likewise find themselves in diverse fields—education, business, science, arts—where faithful stewardship can foster widespread positive change.

Living as salt and light

Jesus' teaching in Matthew 5:13–16 describes believers as "the salt of the earth" and "the light of the world." Salt preserves and flavors; light dispels darkness and reveals truth. Embracing this call entails ethical conduct, compassion, and creative problem-solving that reflect God's character in secular settings. A Christian executive might institute fair labor practices that protect workers' dignity, or an artist might create works that challenge societal ills while pointing to redemption. By embodying biblical values in our professional arenas, we become catalysts of transformation that align society more closely with God's justice and righteousness.

Influence through excellence

One means of societal influence is excellence in your field. Daniel excelled so thoroughly that the Babylonian officials could find no fault in his work (Daniel 6:4). Likewise, whether you're a teacher, engineer, entrepreneur, or stay-at-home parent, pursuing excellence can earn credibility. This credibility opens doors for respectful conversation about the motivation behind your diligence—namely, your love for God and neighbor. By producing top-quality work, believers display integrity and dedication that stand out in a world often preoccupied with shortcuts or self-interest. Over time, this ethos can reshape organizational cultures, policies, and community standards.

Advocating for justice and mercy

A chosen life also involves advocating for the vulnerable. Micah 6:8 encapsulates God's heart, calling His people "to do justice, and to love kindness, and to walk humbly" with Him. Today, social structures frequently disadvantage certain groups—ethnic minorities, the poor, refugees, children without stable homes, or individuals with disabilities. If you feel burdened for such injustices, that burden might be part of your calling. Practical engagement could include volunteering at a crisis center, influencing legislation, offering pro bono services in legal, medical, or counseling fields, or developing innovative community programs. By championing justice and mercy, believers reflect the compassion of Christ and pave the way for holistic transformation.

Kingdom-minded partnerships

Societal impact often requires collaboration across denominational and organizational lines. Partnerships between churches, nonprofits, businesses, and government agencies can achieve more than isolated efforts. If your calling resonates with transforming specific societal spheres—like education reform or environmental stewardship—seek out like-minded believers and organizations. Paul repeatedly acknowledged his co-laborers in the gospel (Romans 16:3–4), demonstrating that synergy accelerates kingdom advance.

Conclusion

Pursuing a called and chosen life means more than simply

identifying a personal dream or devoting your weekends to volunteer work. It involves a profound alignment with God's redemptive storyline, acknowledging that He both invites (calls) and appoints (chooses) individuals to fulfill roles intricately woven into His larger plan. When you embrace this identity—whether serving in a local congregation, advocating for justice in the secular realm, or quietly tending to daily responsibilities with faithfulness— you embody a life that transcends self-interest, drawing purpose and power from the One who set you apart.

As you conclude this chapter, consider pausing for a moment of reflection:

- Have I truly sought God's direction for my life, beyond generic career goals or cultural expectations?

- Am I open to the possibility that God may choose me for tasks I feel unqualified or even reluctant to undertake?

- In what areas of the Church or wider community might my gifts and burdens intersect with pressing needs?

Praying over these questions can yield fresh insights into your next steps. And remember, the ultimate aim is not personal fame or comfort but the glorification of Christ, who deserves the honor that flows from lives fully surrendered to His will. Such lives, grounded in calling and choice, form a shining testimony that Jesus is Lord, and His kingdom is worth our absolute devotion. May you walk this path with courage, humility, and expectancy, knowing that a life entrusted to God's hands is never wasted—but woven into a divine masterpiece whose impact echoes throughout eternity.

Chapter 9: Prophecy vs. Covenant: Understanding God's Promises

From the earliest biblical records, God reveals Himself as One who initiates a relationship with humanity, communicates His plans, and establishes enduring promises. Two of the most pivotal vehicles for this revelation are prophecies—inspired declarations about God's intentions or future events—and covenants—binding agreements that define the terms of the relationship between God and humanity. Because prophecy and covenant appear throughout the Scriptures, they form crucial threads in the biblical tapestry, unveiling God's unchanging character and His redemptive plan.

Yet prophecy and covenant are often misunderstood or merged into a single concept. *Prophecy* can evoke images of cryptic predictions or fiery preachers foretelling doom. *Covenant*, meanwhile, might sound like an archaic legal term or remain vaguely synonymous with "promise." In reality, each has a distinct function that illuminates who God is, what He is doing in history, and how believers are to respond to His directives. Understanding these distinctions—and how they connect—can strengthen one's faith, clarify biblical interpretation, and foster a deeper trust in God's integrity.

In this chapter, we will explore foundational concepts that differentiate prophecy and covenant, analyze the principles for interpreting prophetic revelation, examine the lasting relevance of covenant promises for today's believers, and learn how to live confidently in light of God's unbreakable word. Though at times complex, this subject provides a powerful window into God's heart, demonstrating His desire to guide, redeem, and dwell with His people. May you emerge with renewed awe at God's faithfulness, equipped to receive His promises with both humility and hope.

9.1. Foundational Concepts

9.1.1 Prophetic Messages and Their Purpose

Biblical prophecies in a nutshell

In Scripture, a "prophecy" is a message conveyed by a prophet—someone uniquely commissioned to speak on God's behalf. This message may involve prediction of future events, direct confrontation of present sin, or comfort to a weary community. Prophets such as Elijah, Isaiah, Jeremiah, and Amos exemplify individuals who delivered divine warnings and reassurances. Not all prophecy is predictive; some are more accurately *forth-telling* (articulating God's truth and call to repentance) than *foretelling* (announcing events yet to occur). A prophet's job is thus multi-faceted: to reveal God's viewpoint on current issues and, when relevant, to offer glimpses of His plans for the future.

Clarifying the role of prophecy

At times, modern audiences reduce prophecy to fortune-telling, seeking a secret "road map" for personal guidance. However, the scriptural model emphasizes that prophecy is primarily an instrument of revelation, correction, and encouragement. In 2 Chronicles 20:20, King Jehoshaphat admonishes Judah, "Believe in the LORD your God, and you will be established; believe His prophets, and you will succeed." Here, prophecy is not presented as mere mysticism but as a life-giving word that calls God's people to align with His perspective. Similarly, 1 Corinthians 14:3 explains that prophecy in the New Testament context is for "upbuilding and encouragement and consolation." At its essence, prophecy draws people closer to God, shedding light on His will and urging them to respond in faith.

Prophecy and the integrity of God's Word

Scriptural prophecies underscore that God's Word is reliable. For instance, the prophet Isaiah proclaims, "The former things I declared of old; they went out from My mouth, and I announced them; then suddenly I did them, and they came to pass" (Isaiah 48:3). This statement highlights a divine pattern: God declares in advance what He will do, then fulfills it precisely, validating His sovereignty and truthfulness. This pattern fosters trust among God's people, who see that He is neither capricious nor dishonest. Prophecy thus stands as a visible sign that God rules history and that His words deserve reverent attention.

Warnings and hope

Biblical prophecy frequently combines warnings with assurances of future redemption. For example, the prophet Amos warns Israel of impending judgment if they persist in injustice (Amos 2:6–8; 4:1–2). Yet the same book ends with a promise of restoration (Amos 9:11–15). In Jeremiah, strong announcements of exile are paired with promises of a renewed heart and a brighter future (Jeremiah 24:6–7). These dual themes reflect God's consistent character: He is holy and just, requiring repentance, but also merciful and faithful, offering grace to those who turn back to Him.

Relevance for believers

Believers today often encounter "prophetic messages" in various forms—spoken words at church, personal impressions in prayer, or widely circulated claims of revelations about world events. Discerning which messages genuinely reflect God's truth remains essential (cf. 1 Thessalonians 5:19–21). Nonetheless, biblical prophecy encourages us that God continues to guide and shape history for His glory. Recognizing the scriptural framework for prophecy—its moral dimension, its focus on aligning believers with God's righteousness—can anchor us amid competing voices, helping us remain open to legitimate prophetic direction while resisting sensationalism.

9.1.2 Covenants as God's Commitment

Definition of covenant

A covenant, in biblical terms, is a binding agreement between two parties, often formalized through ritual or legal stipulations. Far more than a casual promise, a covenant involves solemn commitment, mutual responsibilities, and overarching blessings or consequences. Biblical covenants typically originate from God, who unilaterally establishes the terms under which humans can relate to Him. For example, God's covenant with Noah (Genesis 9:8–17) included a promise never again to flood the entire earth, symbolized by the rainbow. These divine covenants demonstrate God's proactive love, guaranteeing His faithfulness even when humanity falters.

Major covenants in Scripture

The Bible recounts several pivotal covenants:

1. **Noahic Covenant**: After the Flood, God vowed to preserve life on earth, reinforcing His care for creation (Genesis 9:12–16).

2. **Abrahamic Covenant**: God promised Abraham land, and descendants, and that through him "all the families of the earth shall be blessed" (Genesis 12:1–3; 15:1–21).

3. **Mosaic Covenant**: Through Moses, God gave Israel the Law, with blessings for obedience and curses for disobedience (Exodus 19:5–6).

4. **Davidic Covenant**: God pledged to establish David's dynasty, culminating in an eternal throne (2 Samuel 7:12–16).

5. **New Covenant**: Prophesied in Jeremiah 31:31–34 and inaugurated by Jesus, this covenant promises a transformed heart and direct relationship with God, anchored in Christ's atoning sacrifice (Luke 22:20).

These covenants reveal distinct aspects of God's character—His mercy, holiness, patience, and redemptive purpose. Each covenant forms a milestone in God's progressive unveiling of His plan, culminating in the New Covenant, where the law is written on believers' hearts, not just on tablets of stone.

God's covenantal faithfulness

Throughout Scripture, God's covenants reflect His unwavering faithfulness, even when humans breach their obligations. Israel repeatedly violated the Mosaic Covenant by idolatry and injustice, incurring exile (2 Kings 17:7–18). Yet God preserved a remnant and renewed His people (Ezra 9:8–9). In the Abrahamic Covenant, Sarah's barrenness threatened God's promise of descendants, but He miraculously enabled her to conceive Isaac (Genesis 21:1–2). These patterns illustrate that divine covenants are not precarious bargains but reliable expressions of God's enduring commitment. Though He permits consequences for sin, He consistently advances the covenant promises toward fulfillment.

Unconditional vs. conditional elements

Many biblical covenants contain both unconditional and conditional elements. For example, the Davidic Covenant in 2 Samuel 7 includes unconditional promises about an eternal kingdom, yet David's successors are warned that disobedience will bring chastisement (2 Samuel 7:14). The Abrahamic Covenant is rooted in God's grace, though Abraham's faith and obedience catalyze the unfolding of blessings (Genesis 22:16–18). This tension underscores that while God's overarching plan remains unstoppable, personal participation in covenant blessings often depends on human response. The covenant reveals God's overarching design, while the choices of individuals or nations can influence how they experience its benefits or penalties.

Contrast with secular contracts

A modern contract typically involves equal parties negotiating terms. By contrast, biblical covenants are divinely initiated, with God setting the framework for human acceptance. They pivot on God's grace rather than symmetrical bargaining. Moreover, while secular contracts can be dissolved by mutual agreement or legal loopholes, biblical covenants endure because they rest on God's immutable word. This distinction reassures believers that covenantal security transcends human limitations, pointing to a God who does not lie or rescind His promises (Numbers 23:19).

9.2. Interpreting Prophetic Revelation

9.2.1 Historical Context and Fulfillment

Prophecy rooted in real events

A careful reading of biblical prophecy shows that each message arose within a specific historical setting. Isaiah, for example, ministered in the context of Assyrian expansion, warning Judah of judgment and foretelling the eventual redemption (Isaiah 7:1–17; 10:5–19). Jeremiah prophesied during the final days of the kingdom of Judah before the Babylonian exile (Jeremiah 25:8–11). Understanding these backdrops reveals the immediate significance of the prophecy for the original audience. Rather than random predictions, these oracles functioned as incisive commentary on current socio-political or spiritual conditions, showing God's active involvement in human affairs.

Multiple layers of fulfillment

Biblical prophecies often display multiple layers of fulfillment. For instance, certain passages in the Book of Daniel address both immediate historical crises (conflicts with pagan empires) and far-reaching events that shape end-times expectations (Daniel 2; 7–9).

The concept of near and far fulfillment is evident in Isaiah 7:14. While a child named Immanuel in Isaiah's day served as an immediate sign to King Ahaz, the New Testament sees this prophecy culminating in the birth of Christ (Matthew 1:22–23). This "telescoping" effect underscores God's ability to speak through an ancient scenario while pointing to a grander, often messianic horizon.

Prophetic language and symbolism

Prophetic literature often employs vivid imagery, metaphors, and symbolic actions. Ezekiel's dramatizations—like lying on his side for a prolonged period to represent Israel's iniquity (Ezekiel 4:4–6)—convey God's message in memorable ways. Apocalyptic sections in Daniel or Zechariah depict beasts, horns, or elaborate visions signifying kingdoms and powers. These symbols require careful interpretation, guided by cross-references within Scripture and an understanding of ancient literary forms. Overly literal readings may distort the text, while excessively allegorical approaches risk disregarding genuine historical or future implications. Striking a balance means respecting the prophet's original context and following clues within Scripture itself.

The challenge of predictive prophecy

Predictive prophecies—those foretelling events far in the future—can be subject to misinterpretation or exploitation. In biblical times, false prophets arose, delivering soothing messages or sensational predictions that ultimately proved untrue (Jeremiah 14:13–16). Deuteronomy 18:21–22 provides a test: if a supposed prophecy fails to materialize, the speaker is not a true prophet of the LORD. Today, similar principles apply. Some modern interpreters set rigid timelines for end-times events, risking disillusionment if those forecasts fail. A humble approach acknowledges that while certain prophecies have literal fulfillment (like Christ's birth in Bethlehem, Micah 5:2), others involve timing or details that God alone fully comprehends (Acts 1:7). Recognizing partial or progressive fulfillment prevents sensationalism and encourages reliance on God's sovereign timing.

Messianic prophecies

A significant subset of biblical prophecy pertains to the Messiah—God's anointed deliverer. Passages in Isaiah, Micah, Zechariah, and Psalms prefigure aspects of the Messiah's life, suffering, triumph, and eternal reign. For believers, Christ is the ultimate fulfillment of these prophecies, as the One who embodies "the spirit of prophecy" (Revelation 19:10). Understanding how the Old Testament prophets foresaw a coming King who would inaugurate God's kingdom, heal the brokenhearted, and establish an everlasting covenant brings coherence to the overarching story of redemption.

9.2.2 Principles for Discernment

Examining scriptural alignment

When encountering prophetic claims, either from historical writings or contemporary sources, believers must evaluate them against biblical truth. God never contradicts His revealed Word (Galatians 1:8). Prophecies that advocate moral compromise, deny the deity of Christ, or distort the gospel message should be dismissed. Even well-intentioned utterances must align with core doctrines such as salvation by grace through faith, the lordship of Christ, and the call to holiness. This scriptural yardstick ensures that believers stay anchored to the unchanging foundation of God's self-disclosure.

Testing the fruit

Jesus taught that one discerns false prophets by examining their fruit: "Grapes are not gathered from thornbushes, nor figs from thistles, are they?" (Matthew 7:16–20). While mistakes or sins can occur even among genuine ministers, habitual deception, greed, or unrepentant immorality typically signals that someone is not speaking under God's inspiration. Conversely, a consistent lifestyle of integrity, humility, and biblical fidelity offers a strong indication that a person's prophetic insights warrant consideration. This principle encourages a healthy skepticism of charismatic personalities who fail to demonstrate genuine Christlike character.

Contextualizing prophecy for edification

Paul's guidelines for church gatherings in 1 Corinthians 14 emphasize that prophecy should build up the body of Christ, not sow confusion or fear. Believers should weigh what is spoken, gleaning what edifies and discarding what is questionable (1 Corinthians 14:29). Similarly, any application of prophecy must resonate with the overarching mission of the Church—proclaiming the gospel, discipling believers, and manifesting the love of Christ. If a prophecy incites division, fosters pride, or distracts from the gospel, it likely deviates from the Holy Spirit's intent.

Humility and partial knowledge

Prophetic discernment requires humility, recognizing that "we see in a mirror dimly" (1 Corinthians 13:12). Even legitimate prophecies may be misapplied if individuals interpret them rigidly or inflexibly. Throughout biblical history, prophets themselves had incomplete understanding of the full scope of their messages (1 Peter 1:10–12).

Accepting that our grasp of future details is finite fosters dependence on God. We remain open to correction, mindful that the actual unfolding of events may differ from our assumptions. This stance can help believers avoid dogmatic stances that cause division or overshadow Christ's call to unity.

A posture of watchfulness

Lastly, biblical prophecy encourages an attitude of watchfulness toward God's ongoing work. While the exact day or hour of certain prophecies' fulfillment may remain hidden, believers are exhorted to stay spiritually alert, living in righteousness and readiness (Matthew 24:42–44). True prophetic discernment is thus less about trying to decode timelines and more about aligning with God's heart, pursuing holiness, and participating faithfully in His present and future purposes. In a world tempted by curiosity and sensational headlines, the best approach is careful, prayerful watchfulness undergirded by love and obedience.

9.3. Relevance of Covenant Today

9.3.1 Application to Personal Faith

Living under the New Covenant

While believers honor the legacy of biblical covenants with Noah, Abraham, Moses, and David, they stand primarily under the blessings of the New Covenant, sealed by Christ's sacrificial death and resurrection (Luke 22:20). This covenant surpasses its predecessors by granting an internal transformation, as prophesied in Jeremiah 31:33–34: "I will put my law within them, and I will write it on their hearts." Under this arrangement, believers enjoy direct access to God, no longer confined by the ceremonial shadows of the past (Hebrews 8:6–7, 13). This means that worship is not relegated to a specific temple or sacrificial system but is integrated into every sphere of life, guided by the indwelling Holy Spirit.

Forgiveness and restored relationship

A hallmark of the New Covenant is complete forgiveness of sin (Hebrews 10:16–18). Whereas under the Mosaic Covenant atonement involved repeated animal sacrifices, Jesus offered Himself once for all, thereby removing the need for perpetual rituals. For the believer, this reality unfolds daily as we confess our failings and rely on Christ's sufficiency. Condemnation is replaced by reconciliation, bridging the chasm between a holy God and flawed humanity. Though believers still wrestle with sin, they do so within the embrace of covenant grace, assured that God's favor does not waver with each shortcoming.

Covenantal identity

Being part of God's covenant community shapes identity at its core. First Peter 2:9 depicts believers as "a chosen race, a royal priesthood, a holy nation, a people for his own possession." This collective identity transcends ethnic, social, or national barriers, uniting believers worldwide into a family under one divine Father. It bestows a sense of belonging and purpose: we are not aimless individuals but covenant partners reflecting God's glory. Such identity counters the fragmentation and loneliness often found in secular contexts, providing believers with a stable anchor of significance.

Daily appropriation of covenant promises

Covenant living also entails **appropriating** God's promises daily.

164

While the most sweeping covenant promises concern redemption and eternal life, Scripture includes assurances of guidance (Isaiah 58:11), comfort in trouble (Psalm 46:1), and wisdom for those who ask in faith (James 1:5). Under the New Covenant, these promises find yes and amen in Christ (2 Corinthians 1:20). Rather than viewing them as distant abstractions, believers can approach God's throne of grace with confidence (Hebrews 4:16), trusting His covenant faithfulness in personal struggles, family needs, vocational endeavors, and spiritual growth.

Balancing faith and obedience

The interplay of faith and obedience remains integral to covenant life. While salvation is by grace alone (Ephesians 2:8–9), the New Testament consistently teaches that authentic faith produces good works (Ephesians 2:10). Believers are not saved to remain stagnant but to fulfill the righteous intent of God's law by the Spirit's power (Romans 8:4). This synergy means that, though the New Covenant rescues us from legalistic burdens, it calls for heartfelt obedience flowing from gratitude and love. In effect, covenant living is an ongoing dance of receiving God's unconditional grace and responding with reverent submission.

9.3.2 Continuous Dependence on Divine Assurances

Standing on God's unchanging word

Even under the New Covenant, trials, uncertainty, and spiritual opposition remain part of the Christian journey. In such circumstances, God's covenantal promises act as an unshakable foundation. When Elijah felt isolated and afraid, God reminded him that His plans would endure (1 Kings 19:11–18). Likewise, Paul, beset by hardships, drew strength from Christ's unwavering love

(Romans 8:35–39). For believers today, covenant confidence is not wishful thinking but a tether to the One who cannot lie (Titus 1:2). This bedrock stabilizes faith amid shifting cultural norms or personal adversities.

Receiving guidance and provision

The same God who established covenants in antiquity continues to guide His people. Whether faced with career decisions, relational dilemmas, or moral crossroads, believers can seek God's direction in prayer, trusting He honors His pledge to be our shepherd (John 10:14–15). While external resources—advice from friends, practical tools—are helpful, the Holy Spirit's inner witness often confirms the path forward, echoing the principle of God's covenant presence. Provision, too, flows from this covenant relationship: though we cannot control circumstances, we rely on God's promise that He cares for every need (Philippians 4:19), allowing contentment and generosity to flourish.

Covenant as motivation for perseverance

When discouragement looms, reflecting on covenant promises can reignite perseverance. The apostle Peter, writing to believers under persecution, references God's "precious and very great promises" that enable partakers of the divine nature (2 Peter 1:4). By meditating on these truths, hope stirs anew. Even death, the ultimate human fear, loses its sting under the covenant sealed by Christ's resurrection (1 Corinthians 15:54–57). God's assurance that He will never forsake His own (Hebrews 13:5) propels believers through trials with resilient faith. Day by day, this orientation transforms anxiety into expectancy and resignation into praise.

Renewing covenant awareness

Periodically, it is beneficial for believers to revisit the core covenant truths that anchor their faith. Just as Israel rehearsed their deliverance from Egypt during Passover, modern Christians can reflect on their personal testimonies of salvation, remembering how God intervened to rescue them from sin. Celebrating communion (the Lord's Supper) also reinforces covenant awareness, as we recall Christ's words, "This cup...is the new covenant in my blood" (1 Corinthians 11:25). Such repeated observances cultivate gratitude, humility, and vigilance, ensuring that our reliance on covenant grace remains fresh and life-giving.

9.4. Living in Light of God's Promises

9.4.1 Encouragement Amid Uncertainty

Navigating trials with prophetic hope

Prophecy, understood in its biblical sense, is not merely about deciphering the future but about finding assurance that God is in control. Prophets like Habakkuk wrestled with the question of why evil seemed to prevail, yet concluded with a triumphant declaration of trust: "Though the fig tree should not blossom...yet I will rejoice in the LORD" (Habakkuk 3:17–18). Such confidence rests on the prophetic revelation that God's plans extend beyond immediate hardships. For believers under financial pressure, relational strife, or societal upheaval, recalling that God has already outlined the final chapters of redemption fosters hope amid chaos.

Cultivating a steadfast spirit

Uncertainty often tempts us to doubt God's goodness or question His timing. In these seasons, biblical accounts of prophecy and covenant offer a steadying influence. Consider how the exiles in

Babylon must have felt when Jeremiah prophesied about a future restoration that seemed impossible (Jeremiah 29:4–14). Or how the disciples grappled with Jesus' prediction of His crucifixion, followed by resurrection (Mark 8:31–33). In each scenario, trust in God's unwavering promises brought clarity. By consistently rehearsing these divine assurances—through Scripture reading, worship, and prayer—believers cultivate a steadfast spirit unshaken by the unpredictability of life.

Walking by faith, not by sight

Paul's exhortation to "walk by faith, not by sight" (2 Corinthians 5:7) resonates with both prophecy and covenant. If we only trust what we can see, we may succumb to despair when outward circumstances deteriorate. But when we anchor ourselves in God's pronouncements—His covenant vow to never leave us (Matthew 28:20), His prophetic affirmations that Christ will one day reign in full glory (Revelation 11:15)—we transcend the limitations of the present. This perspective does not ignore reality; rather, it interprets reality through the lens of God's overarching plan. Such faith ignites courage to remain faithful, even when immediate prospects appear bleak.

Comfort in communal lament

Believers walking in covenant sometimes find themselves in collective trials—economic downturns, natural disasters, or persecution. Scripture underscores the value of communal lament: entire communities in the Old Testament fasted, wept, and sought God's deliverance (Joel 2:12–17). Their prayers often referenced previous covenant acts, reminding God (and themselves) of the relationship He established with them. Today, corporate prayer gatherings, intercessory networks, or simply believers uniting across denominational lines can amplify hope. Sharing burdens fosters solidarity, reinforcing that the God who made and fulfilled covenants in the past remains active now.

Patience and perspective

A vital fruit of living in light of God's promises is patience. Abraham waited decades for the birth of Isaac, guided only by God's covenant word (Romans 4:18–20). Prophecies about the Messiah spanned centuries before Christ's advent (1 Peter 1:10–12). Such examples remind us that God's timeline often stretches beyond human expectations. By embracing a long-view perspective, shaped by prophecy's far-reaching scope and covenant's endurance, believers learn to wait well, avoiding hasty decisions or cynicism. Patience, in this biblical sense, emerges from a profound reliance on the One who orchestrates all events for ultimate good (Romans 8:28).

9.4.2 Anticipation and Active Hope

Looking toward ultimate fulfillment

While many biblical prophecies have been fulfilled—such as Christ's first coming or the regathering of Israel after exile—others await final consummation. Passages forecasting the "new heavens and a new earth" (Isaiah 65:17; Revelation 21:1) point to a future in which sin, sorrow, and death are eradicated. This eschatological dimension instills believers with a sense of anticipation. Covenant language affirms that God's people will dwell eternally in His presence, free from the brokenness that currently plagues creation. Such assurance transforms how we view environmental stewardship, moral decision-making, and evangelism, for we recognize that history is moving toward God's glorious renewal.

Hope as an engine for mission

Christian hope is not passive; it fuels mission. The prophet Jonah's reluctance to warn Nineveh (Jonah 1:1–3) contrasts with the Great Commission, where Jesus sends His disciples to make disciples of all nations (Matthew 28:18–20). Because we trust God's promise that the gospel will bear fruit among all peoples (Revelation 7:9–10), we can labor with expectancy. Even in hostile contexts, believers persist, convinced that God's Word will not return void. This conviction that God's kingdom is both present and advancing fosters perseverance in sharing Christ's love and message, confident that prophecy and covenant underscore His unstoppable plan of salvation.

Holiness shaped by promises

Prophecy and covenant remind us that we are not living for the moment but for an eternal kingdom. This perspective refines our ethics. Since we anticipate a future where righteousness dwells (2 Peter 3:13), we strive for holiness now, letting go of corrupt practices that conflict with God's character. Covenant identity underscores that we belong to a holy God, spurring us to reject complacency. Whether it involves ethical business practices, relational purity, or generosity in resource management, an active hope in God's promises challenges us to embody the values of the coming kingdom here and now.

Channels of Divine Blessing

Active hope also manifests in acts of compassion and mercy. Just as the Abrahamic Covenant intended for all nations to be blessed through Abraham's descendants (Genesis 12:3), believers today serve as conduits of grace in their communities. Through feeding the hungry, advocating for social justice, or championing reconciliation, Christians model the love and justice that God's kingdom will fully reveal. Motivated by the knowledge that Christ's reign will eliminate suffering and oppression, believers become catalysts for glimpses of that reign in the present. Their efforts, even if imperfect, anticipate the ultimate shalom that prophecy envisions.

Living covenantally each day

Ultimately, living in light of God's promises entails integrating covenant principles into daily rhythms. Prayer ceases to be a rote ritual and becomes a conversation with the Covenant-Maker. Decision-making flows from a desire to honor the One who binds Himself to us in steadfast love. Worship emerges not merely from tradition but from a heart enthralled by the breadth of God's plan, as revealed through prophecy and sealed by covenant. This daily alignment fosters spiritual vitality, creativity in service, and a contagious hope that touches everyone we encounter.

Conclusion

Prophecy and covenant are two pillars underpinning the entire biblical narrative. Prophecy unveils God's voice in specific historical contexts, guiding His people through warnings, exhortations, and revelations of future triumph. Covenant presents His unbreakable commitment, forging a bond with humanity that endures despite human frailty. Both serve as windows into God's character: He is not a distant deity but One who communicates clearly and enters binding relationships with those He loves.

As this chapter ends, let's reflect on how prophecy and covenant might strengthen your personal walk with Christ:

- Do you find yourself anxious about world events or personal crises? Meditate on the biblical examples of prophecy fulfilled, recalling that God remains sovereign and meticulously faithful.

- Are you weary in the Christian journey? Study the covenant promises that assert God's abiding presence and inexhaustible grace. Remind yourself that His Word, once given, never falls to the ground.

- Have you encountered "prophetic" messages or teachings that seem contradictory or extreme? Commit to biblical discernment, testing everything against Scripture's doctrinal core and the fruit of righteous living.

In so doing, you join a long lineage of believers who have trusted God's promises through every epoch—patriarchs, prophets, apostles, and saints who discovered that God's Word stands firm through the ages. Amid changing times, the synergy of prophecy and covenant continues to illuminate our path, stirring us to worship, obedience, and expectancy. May you grasp these truths with deeper conviction, emboldened by the knowledge that heaven and earth may pass away, but God's Word—His promises—shall never fail.

Chapter 10: Follower vs. Disciples: Embracing True Commitment

One of the most striking aspects of Jesus' ministry was the steady presence of people following Him wherever He went—crowds eager for healing, miracles, or wise instruction. And yet, despite their proximity, many of these "followers" drifted away or remained spectators, never fully embracing the transformative journey that Jesus invited them to undertake. In contrast, Jesus poured His life into a smaller group whom He called disciples—men and women committed to learning from Him, obeying His words, and ultimately continuing His mission in the world. Understanding the difference between these two levels of association is crucial for modern believers, lest we imagine that proximity to Christian teaching or involvement in religious activities automatically equates to genuine discipleship.

This chapter examines the distinctions between *merely following* and *truly discipling*, highlighting the transformative nature of discipleship that goes beyond casual interest. We will begin by defining the terms and exploring the characteristics of a mere follower versus the hallmarks of a genuine disciple. Next, we will investigate the commitment and cost of true discipleship, discussing how moving from passive observation to active participation reshapes our priorities. Then, we will delve into the process of developing as a disciple, emphasizing the role of mentoring, intentional learning, and obedience. Finally, we will examine the call to multiply disciples—teaching, training, and leaving a Christ-centered legacy that spans generations. By the end of this chapter, you will be challenged to evaluate your own spiritual posture and encouraged to embrace the depth of relationship and purpose that Jesus extends to His disciples.

10.1. Defining the Terms

10.1.1 Characteristics of a Mere Follower

External interest without internal transformation

The Gospels describe how crowds routinely surrounded Jesus, intrigued by His authority, teachings, or miracles. For instance, Mark 3:7–9 portrays Jesus attracting large numbers, some traveling from afar just to witness Him healing the sick. Yet, many "followers" were motivated by curiosity, desire for physical relief, or fascination with signs and wonders. John 6:2 explains that a great crowd followed Him "because they saw the signs that He was doing on the sick." Their interest, while genuine at some level, did not always translate into full submission to His words. When Jesus began speaking of deeper spiritual truths, many turned back (John 6:66). This exemplifies the difference between outward association with Christ and inward devotion that leads to life change.

Seeking personal gain or convenience

Another hallmark of mere followers is the tendency to seek Jesus for personal benefit—blessings, healings, or solutions to immediate problems—while neglecting the broader call to transformation. The synoptic Gospels recount instances where people approached Jesus for physical healing but never responded to His subsequent teachings on repentance (Matthew 9:27–31; Mark 10:46–52). Such individuals appreciate the benefits of proximity to Jesus but often remain self-focused. They may celebrate a miracle but resist adjusting their lifestyles or values. In modern contexts, a person might attend church exclusively when in crisis, rarely praying or engaging Scripture unless they feel a direct need. This consumer-like mindset reveals a superficial bond with Christ, anchored more in personal convenience than in love for His character or mission.

Minimal sacrifice and limited obedience

Followers in this category exhibit minimal sacrifice. They prefer association without cost, reminiscent of those who relished Jesus' multiplication of the loaves but were scandalized by His teachings on spiritual commitment (John 6:26–29, 60–66). While they might participate in religious gatherings, they shy away from the deeper challenges of living counterculturally. They are quick to celebrate worship events or enjoy fellowship meals but slow to invest in serving others or practicing spiritual disciplines consistently. Their walk with God seldom extends beyond a safe comfort zone, lacking the willingness to face rejection, hardship, or inconveniences for Christ's sake.

Lack of enduring faith

A key element of a mere follower is the absence of enduring faith.

Mark 4:16–17, in the parable of the sower, speaks of seeds sown on rocky ground, representing those who receive the word with joy but quickly fall away when tribulation or persecution arises. This phenomenon is visible in certain individuals who show initial enthusiasm—attending Bible studies, volunteering briefly, or making emotional commitments—yet vanish once personal trials or deeper discipleship demands arise. They lack the root system of deep faith, revealing a fragile connection to Christ that disintegrates under pressure. While these people may still feel attracted to spiritual experiences, they do not persevere through adversity or submit to life-long growth.

External religious identity

Many mere followers adopt a religious identity outwardly, possibly wearing Christian symbols or affiliating with a local church community, but their day-to-day living remains largely unaffected. They might enjoy Christian music or occasionally read a devotional, but their character, relationships, and decision-making processes show little distinctiveness from secular norms. While they might gather in Christian settings, they do not let the power of the gospel shape their ethics, finances, or moral convictions. This superficial alignment with Christianity stems from tradition, social acceptance, or habit rather than personal conviction, resulting in a nominal faith that never matures into discipleship.

10.1.2 Hallmarks of Genuine Discipleship

Surrendered to Christ's Lordship

In contrast, a *true disciple* acknowledges Jesus' lordship and yields to it. While a follower might see Jesus as a teacher or miracle worker, a disciple recognizes Him as both Savior and Master. This acknowledgment compels complete surrender: "Not my will, but Yours, be done." In Luke 9:23–24, Jesus calls His disciples to deny themselves, take up their cross daily, and follow Him. A disciple's decisions—from vocation to relationships, from finances to leisure—reflect a desire to honor Christ, trusting His wisdom above all. This comprehensive submission stands in stark opposition to self-serving approaches, underscoring that discipleship is not an optional add-on but a core identity.

Consistency in obedience and growth

A disciple pursues consistent obedience, understanding that spiritual maturity emerges through abiding in Christ's word. Jesus says in John 8:31–32, "If you abide in my word, you are truly my disciples, and you will know the truth, and the truth will set you free." This abiding posture includes studying Scripture, praying regularly, and cultivating Christlike virtues such as patience, humility, and compassion. While perfect obedience is impossible on this side of eternity, a disciple demonstrates steady progress, repenting swiftly when they stumble. Their life trajectory displays increasing alignment with biblical principles, rather than selective obedience or stagnant faith.

Prioritizing kingdom values

Genuine disciples prioritize *kingdom values* above earthly ambitions. They are not merely interested in personal success, comfort, or recognition, but in seeing God's will advanced. This often translates into radical generosity, servant leadership, and a willingness to stand against societal trends when those trends conflict with the gospel. The Sermon on the Mount (Matthew 5–7) outlines kingdom ethics that challenge disciples to love enemies, refrain from hypocrisy, and store treasures in heaven. While such ideals contrast sharply with worldly norms, a disciple sees them not as suggestions but as guiding principles, shaping how they handle conflict, finances, relationships, and more.

A life marked by love and service

Jesus taught that the distinguishing mark of His disciples is love: "By this all people will know that you are my disciples, if you have a love for one another" (John 13:35). A disciple's love transcends tribalism or personal preference, extending grace and hospitality even to those who differ or oppose them. This love is not sentimental but sacrificial, exemplified in acts of care for the marginalized, forgiveness of offenders, and the unselfish building up of fellow believers. Moreover, disciples steward their gifts to serve, mirroring Jesus who came not to be served but to serve (Mark 10:45). In this way, a disciple experiences the joy that arises from living for others rather than self.

Commitment to Christ's mission

Finally, a genuine disciple embraces participation in Christ's mission—declaring the good news of salvation and making more disciples. At the Great Commission (Matthew 28:18–20), Jesus tasks His disciples with teaching and baptizing in His name. True discipleship involves aligning with this mission. Whether witnessing to co-workers, volunteering in local outreach, or taking the gospel across cultural barriers, disciples see themselves as ambassadors for Christ (2 Corinthians 5:20). They invest their time, resources, and prayers to see others experience the transformative grace they have known. This evangelistic and disciple-making focus stands in stark contrast to mere curiosity or passive attendance.

10.2. Commitment and Cost

10.2.1 Transitioning from Observing to Participating

From the periphery to core involvement

As believers deepen in faith, they move from passive observation—watching, listening, or attending events—to core involvement in the community and mission of the Church. In Mark 3:13–15, Jesus calls the Twelve not just to watch Him but to be "with Him," and He sends them out to preach and cast out demons. This shift embodies the difference between hearing a sermon and being shaped by it, between admiring Christian service and actively engaging in it. A disciple invests wholeheartedly in ministries, relationships, and spiritual practices that cultivate growth, stepping off the sidelines to become an integral contributor to God's work.

Ownership of one's spiritual journey

Transitioning to deeper participation involves owning one's spiritual journey. Many remain stuck in a follower mindset because they rely on others to define or sustain their faith—hoping the pastor, mentor, or worship band will carry them along. In contrast, a disciple takes responsibility for seeking truth, practicing disciplines like Scripture memorization or fasting, and joining small groups for accountability. This self-motivation signifies a shift from consumer to co-laborer with Christ. While church leaders provide guidance, the disciple personally seeks God's presence and invests in spiritual habits that foster Christlike transformation.

Risking vulnerability and authenticity

Participation in the body of Christ calls for vulnerability. Disciples often share testimonies of personal struggles and victories, pray for each other's burdens, and address relational conflicts with truth and grace (Matthew 18:15–17). Shallow followers may attend church sporadically to avoid deep relationships that expose flaws. But disciples recognize that genuine fellowship fosters growth. They choose to be real about temptations, weaknesses, and doubts, trusting that healing and encouragement emerge in an atmosphere of honesty (James 5:16). This vulnerability, while at times uncomfortable, catalyzes spiritual breakthroughs and cement communal bonds.

Influence and responsibility

As one moves from observer to active disciple, influence typically expands. In Acts 6:1–7, the early Church appoints faithful individuals to oversee the distribution of food, solving practical problems while releasing the apostles to focus on prayer and preaching. Taking responsibility—whether in small group leadership, children's ministry, or community outreach—allows disciples to steward gifts for kingdom impact. However, with influence comes accountability. A disciple cannot treat spiritual commitments casually, for people look to them as examples. This accountability further spurs growth, prompting the disciple to remain grounded in prayer, Scripture, and humility.

Spiritual warfare and Perseverance

Deeper involvement can provoke spiritual opposition. When a believer transitions from casual attendance to purposeful service, the enemy often counters with discouragement, temptations, or interpersonal conflicts (Ephesians 6:12). Disciples must respond with vigilance—praying fervently, putting on the armor of God, and surrounding themselves with supportive relationships (Ephesians 6:10–18). They learn perseverance, refusing to quit when faced with setbacks or criticisms. This perseverance fosters robust faith, refining the disciple's character and anchoring their identity in

Christ rather than external validation.

10.2.2 Sacrifice and Personal Growth

The biblical call to sacrifice

Throughout Scripture, those who follow God wholeheartedly embrace sacrifice. Abraham left his homeland at God's command (Genesis 12:1), Ruth forsook her native land to remain loyal to Naomi (Ruth 1:16–17), and the early apostles left behind fishing nets and tax booths (Mark 1:16–20; 2:14). Jesus clarifies that if anyone would come after Him, they must "deny themselves and take up their cross daily" (Luke 9:23). This principle underscores that genuine discipleship is not an addendum to an otherwise worldly lifestyle; it reorients the entire person. The "cross" symbolizes self-denial, a willingness to endure hardship, and even face ridicule or persecution for Christ's sake.

Redefining success

Sacrificial living compels a new definition of success—measured not by wealth, status, or comfort but by faithfulness, obedience, and Christlike service. While the world lauds those who climb professional ladders or accumulate luxuries, disciples weigh their choices differently. They might forgo lucrative opportunities that conflict with biblical ethics or relocate to serve in ministries with modest pay. Though some might call these decisions "unwise" from a worldly standpoint, the disciple discerns that pleasing God outranks personal gain. Their ultimate gauge becomes: *Am I advancing God's kingdom and glorifying Him through my life's direction?*

Transformation through hardship

Personal growth often accelerates amid hardship. Romans 5:3–5 teaches that suffering produces endurance, character, and hope—a progression shaping believers into Christ's image. When disciples face trials—be it financial challenges, relational betrayals, or health crises—they rely on God more profoundly. This dependence cultivates spiritual fortitude, compassion for others, and a deeper grasp of God's faithfulness. Rather than perceiving trials as pointless misfortunes, disciples interpret them as refining processes under the sovereign hand of God (1 Peter 1:6–7). Over time, a track record of perseverance fosters humility and gratitude, hallmarks of mature disciples.

Joy amid sacrifice

Sacrifice does not equate to misery. Paradoxically, disciples often find joy precisely in laying down lesser pursuits for the sake of the gospel. In Acts 5:41, the apostles rejoiced that they were counted worthy to suffer dishonor for Christ's name, reflecting an inner satisfaction that overshadowed public shame. This joy stems from the awareness that they share in Christ's sufferings (Philippians 3:10) and that eternal rewards transcend earthly scorn. Likewise, modern disciples who invest energy in charitable outreach, endure ridicule for biblical convictions or serve in under-resourced contexts frequently testify to an unshakable joy rooted in God's presence. Sacrifice, far from draining them, fuels deeper intimacy with the One they serve.

Continuous re-evaluation

The cost of discipleship is not settled in a single moment; it requires ongoing re-evaluation of priorities. Life circumstances shift—family responsibilities, new job opportunities, health issues—and each season demands discernment about how best to honor Christ. A disciple remains adaptable, willing to revisit assumptions, and remain open to fresh calls from God. Perhaps He asks a busy professional to reduce workload to mentor younger believers or encourages a retiree to devote more time to mission work. In each scenario, sacrifice emerges anew, presenting fresh avenues for personal growth. Through this ongoing process, the disciple cultivates sensitivity to the Holy Spirit's leading, ensuring that their life remains aligned with God's evolving purposes.

10.3. Developing as a Disciple

10.3.1 Intentional Learning and Mentoring

The biblical model of mentoring

Jesus' method of disciple-making involved close relational investment—He spent time teaching, demonstrating, and correcting the Twelve in everyday contexts (Mark 3:14; John 13:1–17). The apostle Paul later replicated this approach, mentoring Timothy and Titus, among others (1 Timothy 1:2; Titus 1:4). This relational model contrasts with purely academic instruction, emphasizing the life-on-life transfer of wisdom. A disciple grows not simply through reading doctrinal statements, but by observing mature believers handle conflict, share faith, or manage finances under biblical principles. The warmth of real examples fosters deeper internalization of godly habits.

Characteristics of a healthy mentoring relationship

A healthy mentoring dynamic involves trust, mutual respect, and a clear goal of spiritual maturity. Typically, the mentor is further along in discipleship—either older in age or more seasoned in faith—and offers counsel, encouragement, and accountability. The mentee, in turn, demonstrates humility, teachability, and initiative, following up on advice and applying biblical counsel. Both should pray for and with each other, forging a safe environment where doubts or struggles can be voiced without fear of condemnation. Over time, this mutual exchange shapes the mentee's character, enabling them to replicate the process by mentoring others eventually (2 Timothy 2:2).

Learning beyond classroom settings

While structured discipleship classes or Bible studies are valuable, effective disciple formation extends beyond formal environments. Jesus taught His disciples along the road, in homes, and during daily tasks, reinforcing that spiritual lessons permeate every sphere of life (Matthew 13:36; 15:15). Similarly, a mentor might invite a mentee to accompany them on errands, serve together in ministry, or discuss Scripture during casual meals. This integrated approach fosters holistic growth: the mentee witnesses biblical principles in real-time decision-making. Learning thus becomes dynamic, illustrating that discipleship is not confined to Sunday mornings but is woven into everyday experiences.

10.3.2 Shaping Character Through Obedience

Obedience as a catalyst

Jesus underscores that those who love Him obey His commands (John 14:15). Obedience is not drudgery but a catalyst for character formation. When believers apply biblical teachings—whether about forgiveness (Luke 17:3–4), sexual purity (1 Thessalonians 4:3–5), or generosity (2 Corinthians 9:6–8)—they discover deeper freedom and transformation. Obedience fosters spiritual "muscle memory," training the mind and heart to respond to life's scenarios

184

with Christ's perspective. Over time, consistent compliance with Scripture uproots old habits, fosters virtues like patience and self-control, and reflects God's holiness to the watching world.

Internalizing biblical values

Beyond legalistic rule-following, true obedience emerges from internalizing God's values. The Holy Spirit works within believers, inscribing the law on their hearts (Hebrews 10:16). This transformation means that disciples obey not merely out of fear of punishment or pursuit of rewards but because they resonate with God's nature. For instance, a disciple refrains from gossip, not just to avoid consequences, but because they see others as created in God's image, deserving respect. This heart-level alignment matures as believers meditate on Scripture, worship, and cultivate intimacy with God, nurturing sincerity rather than mechanical compliance.

Challenges to obedience

Obedience can face multiple obstacles:

- **Peer Pressure**: In workplaces or social circles that prize materialism or immorality, disciples may feel isolated for upholding biblical convictions.

- **Internal Desires**: Past traumas or ingrained addictions can complicate the journey toward obedience, requiring counseling, inner healing, and supportive community.

- **Cultural Messages**: The broader culture may label Christian morals as outdated or intolerant, pressuring disciples to compromise.

In each case, perseverance in obedience underscores reliance on

God's grace and the indwelling Spirit. Failure to obey or a temporary lapse does not disqualify a disciple; rather, it becomes an opportunity for repentance, growth, and renewed dependence on Jesus (1 John 1:9).

Fruit of the Spirit

Paul's depiction of the "fruit of the Spirit" in Galatians 5:22–23 encapsulates the character traits that blossom under sustained obedience. Love, joy, peace, patience, kindness, goodness, faithfulness, gentleness, and self-control naturally flourish when disciples yield to the Holy Spirit's leading. This fruit, in turn, validates one's claim to follow Christ more convincingly than mere words. People outside the Church often become open to the gospel upon witnessing believers who exhibit such virtues even under stress or adversity. Obedience, thus, is not merely a moral duty but a pathway to reflect God's beauty in a fractured world.

10.4. Multiplying Disciples

10.4.1 Teaching and Training Others

The Great Commission's scope

Jesus' final instructions in Matthew 28:18–20 constitute the Great Commission, mandating disciples not just to remain cloistered in personal piety but to go, make disciples of all nations, baptizing them and teaching them to obey all His commands. This commission underscores that every disciple is also a disciple-maker in some capacity. While some are called to cross-cultural missions, others reach families, neighborhoods, or workplaces. The core is the same: reproducing in others the knowledge, faith, and obedience we ourselves have received.

Teaching with authority and grace

Effective disciple-making involves teaching, but not as a mere transfer of information. Jesus taught "as one who had authority" (Mark 1:22), yet He also demonstrated compassion for the weak and the searching (Matthew 9:36). When equipping others, disciples must blend truth (sound doctrine) with grace (patience, empathy). This approach values questions, fosters dialogue, and respects individual learning paces. For instance, a small group leader might guide new believers through foundational doctrines— salvation by grace, the nature of God, the centrality of Scripture— while patiently helping them navigate doubts. Over time, these teachings shape convictions, leading to deeper faith.

Adapting methods for different contexts

Although the gospel message remains unchanging, teaching styles vary across cultures and generations. The early Church taught house to house (Acts 2:46), while Paul often reasoned in synagogues or public marketplaces (Acts 17:17). Today, technology facilitates online Bible studies, while in-person gatherings, retreats, or mentorship lunches remain valuable. A disciple-maker discerns which methods resonate best with the people they serve—youth might benefit from interactive discussions, whereas older adults might prefer systematic studies. Adapting methods, however, does not dilute biblical truth; it simply ensures that the unaltered gospel finds accessible expression in each setting.

Equipping for multiplication

Raising up disciples requires a focus on multiplication rather than merely maintaining a group of perpetual learners. Paul advises Timothy, "What you have heard from me...entrust to faithful men who will be able to teach others also" (2 Timothy 2:2). This chain reaction ensures that each generation of believers invests in the next. Leaders or mentors can promote multiplication by delegating responsibilities—letting emerging disciples lead prayer segments, facilitate Bible discussions, or coordinate outreach events. As these emerging leaders gain confidence and competence, they, in turn, train others. This cascading process mimics how Jesus equipped the Twelve to continue His mission after His ascension.

Avoiding unhealthy dependence

While teaching and training, disciple-makers should guard against unhealthy dependence, where mentees rely exclusively on their mentor's guidance. Instead, the goal is to foster direct intimacy with Christ through personal study, prayer, and reliance on the Holy Spirit. Over time, a healthy mentor releases more responsibility to the disciple, enabling them to initiate their own ministries or lead new believers. This release fosters spiritual maturity rather than stunted growth. Just as a parent gradually steps back so a child can walk, so a disciple-maker eventually steps into a supportive, rather than directive, role, celebrating the disciple's developing leadership.

10.4.2 Building a Legacy of Faith

Discipleship beyond one generation

A vital facet of biblical discipleship is its transgenerational impact. The faith we receive is not ours to hoard; it is a deposit we pass on. Proverbs 13:22 notes, "A good man leaves an inheritance to his children's children," and this principle can be applied spiritually. Parents discipling their children is an obvious avenue, but so is investing in spiritual "children" within the church or community. By establishing a culture of discipleship that values personal transformation, relational mentorship, and communal worship, believers can shape future generations long after they are gone.

Cultivating spiritual legacies in families

Within families, discipleship can integrate devotionals, prayer, or Scripture discussion into daily routines. Deuteronomy 6:6–7 instructs the Israelites to teach God's commands diligently to their offspring—speaking of them when sitting in the house, walking on the road, lying down, and rising. Modern families can adapt these rhythms, discussing Sunday sermons over lunch, praying together each morning or evening, and encouraging children to explore their faith questions openly. By modeling consistent faith at home, parents and guardians leave a blueprint for moral and spiritual decisions. This environment fosters an authentic witness that kids can embrace, thereby perpetuating a heritage of godliness.

Eternal perspective

Finally, building a legacy of faith reminds disciples of an eternal perspective. While secular society often preoccupies itself with short-term gains or immediate gratification, disciple-makers consider how present actions echo into eternity. They realize that each person they lead to Christ, every child taught to pray, and each believer they empower to multiply will have eternal ramifications. For the disciple, the true success lies not in applause or metrics but in seeing lives transformed under the lordship of Jesus, knowing that the seeds sown now bear fruit in God's eternal kingdom.

Conclusion

Throughout this chapter, we have contrasted the difference

between being a follower—someone loosely affiliated with Jesus for personal gain or casual interest—and becoming a disciple, an individual wholly invested in learning from Christ, obeying His commands, and partnering in His redemptive mission. While a follower's involvement remains superficial and often short-lived, a disciple's commitment runs deep, transforming character, priorities, and relationships. Scripture is replete with examples of people who moved from curiosity to conviction, from the periphery to the heart of God's plan, and from nominal faith to vibrant discipleship that changed the course of their communities.

The cost of discipleship is real; it includes self-denial, perseverance under trials, and sacrificial investment of time, resources, and affections. Yet the joy far outweighs the sacrifice, for disciples experience the profound privilege of knowing God intimately, reflecting His love, and contributing to a kingdom that transcends earthly confines. They learn under wise mentors, shape their character through consistent obedience, and eventually replicate these patterns in others, building a legacy of faith that can endure across generations. This is not a passive calling but an active, dynamic journey that enlists every dimension of one's life.

As you reflect on these truths, consider where you stand in the spectrum between *follower* and *disciple*. Do you find yourself lingering in the crowd, observing Jesus from a comfortable distance? Are there areas of your life where you have resisted Christ's invitation to deeper obedience or missed opportunities to invest in others' spiritual growth? The gospel beckons you forward, promising grace for every step of repentance and empowerment for each bold act of service. Whether you're a seasoned believer or someone exploring the faith more recently, God's desire is clear: that you progress beyond mere curiosity into a flourishing discipleship that transforms you from within and radiates outward to bless the world.

May the Holy Spirit guide you to a richer understanding of what it means to be a disciple, empowering you to move beyond the shallows and plunge into the depths of Christ's calling.

www.ingramcontent.com/pod-product-compliance
Lightning Source LLC
Chambersburg PA
CBHW070806050426
42452CB00011B/1912